THE ALIEN INVASION
SURVIVAL HANDBOOK

THE ALIEN INVASION SURVIVAL HANDBOOK

A DEFENSE MANUAL FOR THE COMING EXTRATERRESTRIAL APOCALYPSE

HOW
BOOKS

Cincinnati, Ohio
www.howdesign.com

W.H. MUMFREY

For more fine books from F+W Media, visit www.fwmedia.com.

13 12 11 10 09   5 4 3 2 1

Distributed in Canada by Fraser Direct, 100 Armstrong Avenue, Georgetown, Ontario, Canada L7G 5S4, Tel: (905) 877-4411. Distributed in the U.K. and Europe by David & Charles Brunel House, Newton Abbot, Devon, TQ12 4PU, England, Tel: (+44) 1626-323200, Fax: (+44) 1626-323319, E-mail: postmaster@davidandcharles.co.uk. Distributed in Australia by Capricorn Link, P.O. Box 704, Windsor, NSW 2756 Australia, Tel: (02) 4577-3555

Library of Congress Cataloging-in-Publication Data

Mumfrey, W. H.

The alien invasion survival handbook : a defense manual for the coming

extraterrestrial apocalypse / by W.H. Mumfrey.

     p. cm.

Includes index.

ISBN 978-1-60061-162-9 (pbk. : alk. paper)

1. Extraterrestrial beings--Humor. I. Title.

PN6231.E97M86 2009

818'.607--dc22

                              2008040999

Edited by Lauren Mosko and Scott Francis
Designed by Claudean Wheeler
Illustrations by Ben Patrick
Production coordinated by Greg Nock

This book is dedicated to

ADAM LAMPE,

whose courage during repeated alien abductions
is a true inspiration to humanity.

I would like to offer my sincere thanks to the numerous people who have offered their support and dedicated their valuable time to this project, including Sara Crowe; Lauren Mosko; Amy Schell, Ben Patrick and countless others who have contributed by way of research or involvement in one of the numerous surveys.

THIS CERTIFIES THAT THE SIGNATURE AND PHOTOGRAPH
SPECIAL AGENT *W.H. Mumfrey*
OF FEDERAL BUREAU OF JUSTICE, UNITED STATES DEPARTMENT OF INVESTIGATION

W.H. Mumfrey lives on an island off the south coast of Australia and since applying the prin-ciples in this book he has not been abducted by aliens.

TABLE OF CONTENTS

INTRODUCTION

Since aliens first raised their grotesque heads in H.G. Wells's 1898 novel, *The War of the Worlds*, we have known that when they come, it will not be in peace. And despite the valiant efforts of Hollywood producers, we know that they will not be the benevolent beings so lovingly portrayed in some movies. Their mission won't be to guide us to a higher level of consciousness or to solve our environmental woes.

Many believe that aliens are already here and have, since the dawn of civilization, been inexorably pursing a secret agenda, destroying the lives of people around the world through a regime of abduction and intimidation. Indifferent to our concept of human rights, they have systematically exploited, probed, and violated us— and we are powerless to resist them.

It is time to say enough is enough. We will no longer passively offer ourselves as their intergalactic lab rats. We must take action.

This book is designed to prepare you for the battle of your life.

But how can we possibly fight an enemy that is so ruthlessly efficient, cunningly elusive, and technologically advanced? This book provides you with the answers. In it, you will find the complete step-by-step guide to combating the extraterrestrial menace in day-to-day situations. Want to know how to block alien mind control? Escape from an alien spacecraft? Survive in the vacuum of space? Stave off an alien attack with household appliances? Locate and destroy alien implants? It's all here. Compiled from genuine field research by our network of international experts, the advice offered in this book has been tried and tested during real-life extraterrestrial encounters.

Whether you have yet to encounter an alien or you have been the victim of repeated abductions, this book will provide you with all the necessary skills to defeat these nefarious adversaries and re-gain control of your life. It will be the only book you want in your back pocket when *what if?* becomes *what the hell is that?*

For those of you who think this is all make-believe or just some elaborate hoax designed by bespectacled nerds to fill their time be-tween *Star Trek* conventions, think again. Please answer the following important questions before proceeding any further with this book.

ABDUCTION ASSESSMENT

Have you ever:

- Had the feeling that you were being watched?
- Lost or misplaced common household items, such as TV remote controls, pens, or single socks?
- Seen unusual lights in the sky?
- Discovered mysterious scars on your body that you could not explain?
- Experienced a "lost" period of time (e.g., while driving your car) in which you didn't know where you were or what you had just done over the preceding minutes?
- Felt the sensation of flying while asleep?
- Awoken with a sudden jolt from a deep sleep?
- Woken up with a sense of a strange person or presence in the room?
- Experienced tenderness or soreness in any part of your body without knowing why?
- Felt anxious or agitated for no apparent reason?
- Had feelings of disbelief about aliens or UFOs?

If you have answered *yes* to three or more of these questions, you have probably been abducted by aliens at some time in your life.

Do not be alarmed. You are not the only one. A study by the U.S.-based Roper Organization concluded, "one out of every fifty adult Americans may have had UFO abduction experiences." That adds up to millions of people in the United States alone. Don't panic! Although you have been probed and violated without your knowledge or consent, you now, for the first time, have an opportunity to undo the damage you have received at the hands of our merciless interstellar visitors.

If you answered yes to only one or two of these survey questions, it's only a matter of time before they will come for you. Don't wait until you feel their gangly fingers around your neck to prepare; act now. If you don't protect yourself and your loved ones from the alien menace, who will?

CHAPTER 1

KNOW YOUR ENEMY

> If you know the enemy and know yourself, you need not fear the result of a hundred battles. If you know yourself but not the enemy, for every victory gained you will also suffer a defeat. If you know neither the enemy nor yourself, you will succumb in every battle.
>
> —Sun Tzu

CHAPTER SUMMARY

The first step to overcoming any problem is to acknowledge the problem exists. Knowledge is power. This is never truer than when it comes to our alien adversaries. We must understand our formidable enemy before we have any chance of mounting a defense against them.

Although aliens are more active today than at any other time in Earth's history, they are generally ignored by society, viewed as mere legends and fables, or misrepresented on the silver screen for our entertainment. This mass sense of complacency plays right into their hands. The relentless human harvest that has gone on for millennia continues, unchallenged. Society fails to believe at its own peril.

But if you are reading this book, you have the foresight to perceive the threat, and the guts to take matters into your own hands. Acknowledging the danger is only the first step toward preserving a world free of alien harassment. It is not enough just to recognize an alien if you see one in your backyard. (You don't need a book to help you do that.) To know your enemy is to be intimately acquainted with his intentions, strengths, and weaknesses. Good intelligence is a fundamental principle of any military strategy. Man's greatest fear comes from what he does not know. Once fear is eliminated, you can get down to business, vanquishing our intergalactic foes.

Our preparations must begin by turning the tables on our adversaries and putting them under the microscope. Where do they come from? Why are they here? How are they different than us? It is important that we start by separating fact from fiction. We must peel away the layers of deceit, built over decades of misinformation, to reveal the true identity of our enemy. For it is only by so doing that we discover the chink in their armor through which they can be defeated.

MYTH VS. REALITY

History is littered with accounts of alien visitation (see Appendix A: A Brief History of Resistance). From the very earliest times, humans have recorded in art, word, and print the "terror which comes from the skies." Close encounters with aliens invariably leave an indelible impression upon all those who experience them, inspiring both awe and overwhelming dread. In recent years, Hollywood has portrayed aliens in a multitude of forms, from sadistic, intergalactic monsters to cute, amiable creatures that would make the perfect family pet. Although some moviemakers have come close to the truth with their portrayal of our celestial visitors, most have presented fanciful creatures that bear no resemblance to reality. These images have clouded our perception and distracted us from an insidious presence that threatens each and every one of us.

Truth mixed with error can create an incapacitating state of confusion. It is important that we make a clear distinction between what is pure fantasy and what could be looking in your window at this very moment.

THE ALIEN INVASION SURVIVAL HANDBOOK

FACT FILE # *16734XR-06*

FACT FILE NAME: *Classification of Alien Encounters*

INCIDENT REPORT:

Dr. J. Allen Hynek, a distinguished astronomer and professor, was hired by the U.S. Air Force as a senior scientific adviser on three official unidentified flying saucer ▇▇▇▇▇▇ studies running between 1947 and 1969 (Project Sign, Project Grudge, and Project Blue Book). Although at first a skeptic, his opinions began to change as he examined hundreds of ▇▇▇▇▇▇ UFO reports. Many sightings were reported by reliable witnesses, including fellow astronomers, police officers, military personnel, and civil pilots. In his 1972 book, The UFO Experience: A Scientific Inquiry, Hynek outlines the now-famous classification system used to describe UFO sightings.

CLOSE ENCOUNTERS

OF THE FIRST KIND: A visual sighting of one or more UFOs

OF THE SECOND KIND: Physical evidence of an alien visitation

OF THE THIRD KIND: A sighting of one or more UFO occupants

THE HOLLYWOOD ALIEN

Aliens have regularly appeared on the silver screen since the very inception of cinema in the late nineteenth century. Visionary writer and director Georges Méliès first portrayed them in 1902 in the black-and-white French film *Le Voyage dans la Lune* (*A Trip to the Moon*). This silent, fourteen-minute movie, considered by many to be the first science-fiction film, was loosely based on two popular novels of the time: H.G. Wells's *The First Men in the Moon* (1901) and Jules Verne's *From the Earth to the Moon* (1865). In the film, aliens, known as Selenites, are sublunar stick-insect-like creatures that are hostile to humanity's interests.

This theme of interspecies enmity recurs in the majority of alien films created over the last century. With such notable interstellar villains as H.R. Giger's biomechanical nightmare in Ridley Scott's *Alien* (1979) and the aquaphobic chameleons of M. Night Shyamalan's *Signs* (2002), the diverse representation of alien life-forms are united by the common goal of exploiting humanity. While the fertile minds of Hollywood are, to a large extent, responsible for much of the misinformation that exists in the community about the true nature of extraterrestrials, recent representation of "the grays" in a variety of productions has been closer to the truth than many filmmakers may care to think. If anything, Hollywood should be thanked for inadvertently raising public awareness of the threat posed by aliens.

When it comes to depicting aliens in movies, it is important we remember that the primary focus of Hollywood is on providing the public with entertainment, not education. We must peel away the celluloid veil of deception to reveal the true nature of our extraterrestrial adversaries.

COMMON HOLLYWOOD ALIEN MYTH-CONCEPTIONS

For more than fifty years, Hollywood has been an unintentional source of misinformation about aliens. In an effort to scare and entertain us, they have presented a vision of extra-terrestrials that draws from our most primitive fears. A plethora of fantastic cinematic images have been created that are closer to the dragons and monsters of our ancestral past than they are to reality. These fictions must be uncovered for what they are if we are to be prepared to meet an adversary far more insidious and cunning than the imagination of humans can devise.

- Aliens do not have acid for blood.
- Their young do not gestate within the human body.
- They are not benevolent spiritual beings trying to guide us to a higher plain of consciousness.
- They are not responsible for the majority of crop circles.
- They cannot "shape shift" or "morph" into other forms.
- They are not spawning hybrid alien-human babies.
- They are not responsible for mysterious disappearances of aircraft and ships in the Bermuda Triangle.
- They are not secretly colluding with government agencies.
- They cannot read your mind.
- They cannot levitate.
- They cannot materialize in your room.
- They cannot move objects with their minds.
- They were not responsible for the "face on Mars."
- They cannot be vanquished by a glass of water.
- They do not come in peace.

We need not fear fictional monsters conjured from the dark corners our imagination. The truth is far more disturbing and dangerous. Understanding the terrible truth is the first step to creating a safer world—a world free of extraterrestrial tyranny.

THE ALIEN INVASION SURVIVAL HANDBOOK

FACT FILE # *1673zXR-12*

FACT FILE NAME: *Crop Circles*

INCIDENT REPORT:

Crop circle, or agriglyph, is a term used to describe patterns created by the flattening of a variety of commercial crops, such as wheat, corn, barley, and rye. They range from simple circular shapes to elaborate geometrical formations that stretch for hundreds of yards.

Simple circular shapes have appeared on farmland for countless generations. They have long been attributed to either supernatural forces or natural causes, such as abnormal wind vortices. Since coming to widespread public attention in the 1970s, several thousand crop circles have been documented around the world. Although mass hoaxing is the generally accepted explanation for crop circles, there are still many who believe that they represent a complex form of extraterrestrial communication.

ALIENS 101: ANATOMY AND PHYSIOLOGY

Late one night in 2006, a heavy-vehicle accident on the outskirts of Pine City, Minnesota, resulted in classified military documents being recovered from roadside wreckage by unnamed members of the public. These sensitive documents revealed the range and extent of government interaction with extraterrestrials over the last century. Here, for the first time, we reveal a small portion of the information contained in those recovered files. The public interest is always best served by full disclosure of the facts.

ONE SPECIES

Contrary to the opinions of many UFO enthusiasts, there is only one species of alien proven to be in regular contact with our planet. These have, in recent years, been popularly known as "grays," because of their pallid skin color. There is no way of knowing what they call themselves, due to our inability to effectively communicate with them. Government authorities often refer to them as Extraterrestrial Biological Entities (EBEs).

PHYSICAL CHARACTERISTICS AND ORGAN PROCESSES

As biological entities, aliens are in many ways similar to humans. They breathe the same air we do, must take sustenance, reproduce, and die. Yet, despite the similarities, there are some very imporant fundamental differences. It is, in fact, these differences that have provided aliens with the biological advantage over us in personal combat. When these differences are fully understood, they provide the key to thwarting an enemy who has hitherto seemed invulnerable.

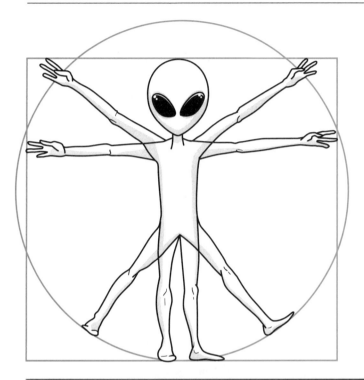

IDENTIFICATION GUIDE

HEIGHT: 3.5–4 feet

WEIGHT: 70–80 pounds

POSTURE: bipedal, fully erect stance and gait

SKIN: light gray to pale blue-gray, hairless

GENERAL DESCRIPTION: Humanoid in appearance. Large, forward-facing eyes, adapted for nocturnal lifestyle. Elongated head with large cranial cavity (2,000–2,500 cc), poor facial mobility and vocal repertoire. Absence of external ears. Small nasal opening. Poorly developed sense of smell. Elongated neck. Long arms relative to leg size; gracile/slender. Four digits; each hand has three fingers and an opposable thumb. Feet have four toes each; all digits are without nails. Sexual monomorphism; no discernable external difference between male and female specimens.

Sense Organs

Sense organs are the parts of the body that receive information from the external environment and convert it into electrical signals that can be interpreted by the brain. Humans have five basic senses: vision, hearing, touch, smell, and taste. Aliens have not only these five, but also a number of unique adaptations that must be studied with due diligence before we can confront our enemies with confidence.

The alien eye and its sight

Alien eyes are similar in structure to our own; they are comprised of a retina, iris, and pupil. However, alien eyes are large and dark, taking up a disproportionate percentage of their faces. Their irises are black, making them indistinguishable from their pupils, which, when fully dilated, are circular. The alien pupil can constrict to thin vertical slits to reduce the amount of damaging daylight entering the eyes. Alien eyes have a translucent nictitating membrane that moves horizontally across the eyeball, giving protection and lubrication. This is often called a "third eyelid" and is common among animals such as birds, lizards, frogs, and some mammals like cats. Humans have a remnant "third eyelid" in the inner corner of the eye. It appears as a small, pink fold of skin and is no longer functional.

Aliens have a thick, reflective membrane behind their retinas, known as the *tapetum lucidum*, which makes their eyes "glow" in the dark in much the same way a dog's or cat's eyes do when you shine a light into them. This special night vision adaptation collects light that has passed through the retina and then reflects it back into the retina, giving the eye a second chance to catch all the available light from dimly lit environments.

All these features make alien eyes specifically adapted to low-light environments, suggesting that they may have evolved on a planet with minimal ambient light. As their eyes are highly sensitive to sunlight, aliens try to restrict their daytime activities as much as possible. It is no coincidence that most alien abductions take place at night.

Studies have shown that aliens have virtually no color vision, they see only in shades of gray. There is also some evidence to suggest that aliens—along with creatures such as certain species of marine life, bats, and birds—perceive ultraviolet (UV) light, which is outside the range of human visibility. As yet, the extent and purpose of this ability remains unknown.

Ears and hearing

It did not take the military scientists of the 1940s long to realize that aliens have only a rudimentary sense of hearing. Early experimentation on captive subjects prior to the Roswell incident (see page 16) revealed little or no response to ambient noises in their surrounding environment. Although, at first, it was thought that they possessed a Zen-like capacity to disassociate from what was happening around them, it was soon discovered that their hearing was impaired to the point of being practically useless.

Aliens also have no external ear structure or pinna. A thin membrane covers the auditory canals, which are situated in slight depressions on either side of the head.

Although they have internal ear structures similar to our own, it is wholly unsuited for our atmospheric air pressure, and, as a result, they are unable to hear many subtle sounds that we take for granted. This is similar, in many ways, to our own partial loss of hearing if we quickly ascend or descend a mountain. What hearing aliens do have tends to be at the high end of the scale, which would make

THE ALIEN INVASION SURVIVAL HANDBOOK

FACT FILE # *1138RS-16*

FACT FILE NAME: *Roswell*

INCIDENT REPORT:

In the summer of 1947, William "Mac" Brazel discovered some strange debris on the ranch where he worked near Roswell, New Mexico. After reporting it to the local sheriff, the ████████ military was called in to investigate the matter. Speculation about a crash became headline news, with rumors about a UFO and dead aliens being widely circulated. Over the last sixty years, the notoriety of this event has grown to make it one of the most famous UFO cases of all time.

There is, to this day, passionate debate about what actually happen at Roswell. Die-hard conspiracy theorists maintain that a UFO and alien bodies were recovered, with a subsequent official ████████ cover-up. Although the Roswell Army Air Field initially issued a press release stating that they had recovered a "flying disc" from the ranch, the military later claimed it was only a weather balloon. In the mid-1990s, the U.S. Air Force issued a ████████ report in an attempt to finally resolve the mystery. They stated that the debris had come from a top-secret government experiment called Project Mogul, which involved balloons carrying equipment into the upper atmosphere to detect Soviet ballistic missiles and nuclear tests.

normal human speech almost inaudible to them. There has been no evidence to suggest that they can read lips, but it is best to not take any chances.

Some scientists have suggested that, even under the right atmospheric conditions, their auditory system is nothing more than an evolutionary relic. Having developed a range of other "super senses," such as electrogenesis and electroreception (see pages 19-23), that allow them to efficiently communicate, any air-based auditory system has been rendered obsolete.

Unauthorized research carried out on a U.S. military base in Guam in 1982 revealed that aliens do recoil from very loud sounds, and they display some degree of agitation when subjected to prolonged human screaming. It was unclear from the available document abstract whether these reactions in any way related to their hearing ability.

Evidence from documents smuggled out of the former Soviet Union during the 1970s indicated that some captured alien specimens have been found fitted with electronic devices that may compensate for their hearing deficiency. Attempts were made to locate scientists associated with these findings after the Soviet Union's collapse in 1991, but both they and their families had disappeared.

The integumentary and nervous systems and touch

With an ambient body temperature lower than humans, alien skin is cool to the touch, more like a reptile than a mammal. It is hairless, smooth, and elastic—similar to dolphin flesh in texture. While humans shed their skin continually in a relatively unobtrusive process—with more than one million skin cells shed every hour—aliens shed their entire skin as a single piece, once every four to six weeks. This lizard-like process takes less than an hour and leaves behind a hollow, transparent sheath that some researchers have dubbed "alien suits." Their new skin has a higher luster and is more sensitive to stimuli for a week or so after molting.

Experiments have shown that aliens respond to external stimuli in much the same way humans do. The same basic array of sensory receptors throughout their bodies allows them to feel sensations like pain, heat, cold, and pressure. Although the degree to which they experience each of these sensations is difficult to determine, it has been demonstrated in clinical situations that their tolerance levels are significantly different from our own. Aliens are also, as previously mentioned, hypersensitive to light.

Olfactory organs, smell, and taste

Aliens have two narrow nostril slits in roughly the same position as our noses. They are valve-like in structure, controlled by a muscular flap. The natural resting position of the nostril is open, but they can be closed to form a watertight seal. While humans can distinguish between at least ten thousand different smells, laboratory tests have revealed that aliens experience some difficulty telling the difference between even distinctive aromas, such as garlic and citrus. They show no discomfort when exposed to an offensive mixture of biological odors, including vomit, rotting vegetables, body odor, human feces, and burnt hair. Even some of the most pungent smells known to mankind—such as the liquid propane warning agent ethyl mercaptan—evoke limited responses in aliens.

With such an underdeveloped olfactory system, we may also assume that alien taste sensors are equally handicapped, but little scientific evidence currently exists to support this idea.

Super Senses

Aliens possess a number of super senses that humans do not have. These senses are linked to their nonverbal form of communication and represent one of the greatest hurdles in opening an effective dialogue with aliens.

Electrosensory perception

When humans talk, sound waves are collected by the outer ear and channeled along the ear canal to the eardrum, where they are converted to minute vibrations within the inner ear. These vibrations, in turn, create a set of electrical nerve impulses that pass through to the hearing center of the brain, where they are translated into sounds the brain can recognize.

Aliens, however, communicate by a process known as electrosensory perception. They basically bypass the central stages of the human speech process and communicate directly via electrical signals. In a process called *electrogenesis*, these electrical impulses are generated by a series of flat, disc-like electroplate cells stacked like batteries in the large frontal lobes of their craniums. Once generated, these electrical impulses travel silently between aliens and are received by specialized electric receptors also buried within the frontal lobe (*electroreception*). The process is completely inaudible to humans. Note that aliens are not able to "read" each

other's minds. Electrogenic communication is a conscious action similar to talking. Each alien's thoughts are its own until it wishes to communicate them.

These processes of electrogenesis and electroreception are not unknown in the animal kingdom, with many creatures such as electric eels, electric rays, sharks, and platypuses using this biological ability to both produce and receive electrical signals. Laboratory experiments have shown that alien electrical-impulse signals have a relatively short range. As air is a weak medium for conducting electrical signals, aliens must remain within close proximity to effectively communicate with each other without the aid of instruments.

There are numerous accounts of aliens staring into the eyes of their paralyzed victims, often from a distance of only inches. Although this is an extremely disconcerting experience, some have suggested that this is their misguided way of trying to communicate with us. As humans do not have electroreception organs, we are quite incapable of receiving any form of electrical-impulse communication from aliens. Similarly, aliens cannot read our minds by telepathy. (Electrogenic communication could be thought as similar to radio broadcasting; you must have both a transmitter and a receiver to communicate. If either one is missing, there can be no communication.) Even if they could "hear" our thoughts, as alien forms of communication are so foreign and indecipherable to us, it may also be possible that they would experience difficulties interpreting our audio-based language.

Electrical discharges from short distances do, however, often trigger the spontaneous firing of synapses (nerve endings) in the human brain. This can result in random and often confusing images and emotional responses, which many have misinterpreted as direct alien communication.

Electroparalysis

Aliens also have the ability to concentrate the focus of their electro-genic impulses to create a sustained discharge capable of temporar-ily paralyzing humans. This ability has long been known to science and has been fully documented in innumerable abduction reports over the last half-century. The actual process was not understood, however, until research carried out during the early 1990s illumi-nated the underlying science.

Although the exact mechanism responsible for this process still remains largely unknown, laboratory tests have shown that certain externally produced electrical pulses are capable of disrupting the electrical signals carried by the body's nerve cells, thereby preventing messages produced in the brain from getting to the rest of the body.

This process of electroparalysis results in a total loss of voluntary muscle control, leaving the victim defenseless and unable to move. Electroparalysis has no effect on involuntary muscular activity, such as respiration or muscular action.

Paralysis is a temporary phenomenon from which the victim soon recovers after the electrical discharge is discontinued. During the recovery stage, which may last anywhere from one to ten minutes, victims may experience disorientation, nausea, disruption of balance, and a lack of strength and coordination.

ELECTROPARALYSIS RESEARCH: HISTORICAL BACKGROUND

All aliens are capable of emitting electrical impulses that can paralyze humans, yet, in abduction situations, we find that only one or two aliens are usually directly involved in paralyzing their human captives. Dr. Ernest Cunningham, a former research scientist at the Dalgety Institute for Applied Psychology, was the first person to note this phenomenon after recording the experiences of more than 1,500 abductees across three continents in the early 1980s. Cunningham called these aliens "glarers," after a phrase used by one interviewed abductee to describe the aliens that stood silently watching in the background during his medical examinations. It is believed that these onlookers have a special ability and training in electroparalysis and are almost exclusively involved in subduing captive humans. In many ways, this ability could be likened to the innate ability that some people have to play a musical instrument or excel at particular sports. Although born with a genetic gift, aliens can develop their skills to perfection through practice.

Wilson and Curruthers (1989) worked with Cunningham's findings and noted a number of incidents where potential abductees were able either to avoid capture or to escape not long after being abducted. All these incidents involved successfully thwarting alien attempts at electroparalysis.

When these individuals were subsequently located and re-interviewed, it was found that each incident had one factor in common: music, either being played during the abduction attempt or being recalled from memory. This revelation led Wilson and Curruthers's team to launch a study known today as Project Bluebird.

When three live alien specimens were captured in North Africa in early 1992, the Project Bluebird team was granted unprecedented access by government agencies to conduct their studies. Government bodies were exceedingly keen to collaborate with Wilson and Curruthers at the outset of their investigations because of the profound military and law enforcement applications of this technology if fully understood and developed. They believed that it may be possible to create machines capable of reproducing the aliens' electrical discharge, which could be used to render individual or group targets paralyzed in both military combat zones and civil disturbance situations.

The laboratory testing of the incarcerated aliens was carried out in secure locations around Europe and lasted until the death of the final subject in late 1994. Not long after, the team was able to replicate the electrogenic pulse in the lab, thereby eliminating the need for trials on rare live alien subjects.

The results of their investigations were published as the top-secret Bluebird Report. In it, they concluded that the electroparalysis techniques used by aliens to immobilize their captives were not foolproof. Two loopholes were discovered and subsequently named Audio-Phonic Resonance and Audio-Morphic Recall, which will be covered in detail in chapter 2.

STRENGTH, SPEED, AND AGILITY

Aliens' gracile body type and apparent lack of a highly developed muscular system would tend to indicate a sedentary lifestyle. This would be consistent with a technologically advanced society where millennia of minimal physical activity have evolved puny physiques. Yet, despite their somewhat spindly form, they are surprisingly agile.

Many case studies exist of aliens who "ran like a greyhound" or were "too quick to catch." In laboratory tests, aliens have been clocked at speeds of more than 33 miles per hour—that's 6 miles per hour quicker than the fastest human speed ever recorded

FIGURE 1.1: Aliens can achieve speeds of up to 33 mph.

(Donovan Bailey, 1996 Atlanta Olympics, 27.1 miles per hour). The challenge in hand-to-hand combat comes not from the aliens' fighting prowess, but from their nimble footwork and evasive maneuvers, making it almost impossible for you to get your hands on them. When you do, their lithe bodies can slip through your fingers like a cake of soap in a tropical downpour.

It would, however, be a grave mistake to underestimate their strength. Although diminutive in size, they are surprisingly strong and have been known to throw a 180-pound man halfway across a room. Aliens are very confident climbers and are able to scale challenging cliffs with ease. Elevated fortifications should not be considered a deterrent to aliens. Laboratory tests have also revealed that aliens are able to hold their breath under water for upward of twenty minutes by slowing their metabolism down to next to nothing.

DIET

Little is known of the alien natural diet. What facts we do know have been gleaned from the personal anecdotes and observations of abductees. Several accounts indicate that they take sustenance orally. Three abductees of the more than three hundred interviewed for this handbook recounted observing aliens imbibing fluids through short tubes connected to the interior walls of their spacecraft. Whether these fluids were nutritional or recreational in nature, we do not know. A diet consisting predominantly of fluids would be consistent with the alien's weak jaw structure and poorly developed teeth.

Dietary information first came to light from government documents leaked in the late 1950s that recorded military attempts to feed captive aliens. They could not be encouraged to eat any of the foods provided by military scientists and were eventually force-fed via feeding tubes inserted into their esophagi. Subsequent tests on their preferred food types have proven inconclusive, although some have displayed a disquieting preference for warm, vitamized meat. Aliens do not absorb nutrients via osmosis through their skin, as some have suggested. Aliens have one opening, a *cloaca*, through which the digestive, urinary, and reproductive systems empty.

REPRODUCTION AND SEXUAL HABITS

Little will be written here of the reproductive habits of aliens. Suffice is to say that this has been a topic of immense interest to researchers who have labored tirelessly over many years to document the often bizarre sexual habits of captive breeding pairs.

Anyone wishing to further pursue the topic should refer to the definitive works of Dr. Joel Mitsky, Head of Reproductive Biology at the former Soviet School of Applied Biology in Saint Petersburg, Russia.

LIFE SPAN

It is impossible to estimate how long aliens live in a natural state. The longest period of time any single alien has been kept alive in captivity is seven and a half years. Although some aliens adapt well to captive conditions, most show a general decline in health from the moment of their incarceration. Despite the very best efforts of research scientists and physicians, most aliens eventually succumb to a mysterious degenerative condition that attacks their vital organs.

All aliens captured to date have been in the adult phase of their development. Captive breeding pairs, despite being very sexually active, have not, as yet, produced any live offspring.

THERMOREGULATION

Alien body temperatures (59°F [15°C]) are unusually low by mammalian standards, and they show a distinct preference for cooler environments. Many abductees have commented on the distinctly frigid temperatures onboard alien spacecraft. Aliens possess an unorthodox thermoregulatory system that does not involve evaporative heat loss.

Aliens are capable of entering a self-induced state of inactivity by lowering their core body temperature, slowing their heart and breathing, and lowering their metabolic rate. This form of hibernation is an energy-conservation mechanism that can last anywhere from minutes to months. Many aliens have feigned death only to emerge from their torpid state to pounce on their victims during an unguarded moment. They can also consciously lower their skin temperature to match ambient air temperature, making them nigh impossible to detect with thermal imaging equipment.

THE ALIEN INVASION SURVIVAL HANDBOOK

FACT FILE # *1673zXR-05*

FACT FILE NAME: *Alien Circadian Rhythms*

INCIDENT REPORT:

Circadian rhythms are the internally generated cycles in the biological processes of all living things. These cycles determine many of our basic biochemical, behavioral and physiological processes, including sleep and feeding patterns. Circadian rhythms were set in the earliest stages of our evolution, being shaped by the dominant environmental cycles of night and day, which on our planet happen to be a twenty-four-hour period, or "about a day," which is the original translation of the phrase (in Latin, circa means "around," dies means "day").

Cyanobacteria	Rabbit	Goldfish	Human	Chipmunk	Alien
22 hrs	23.9 hrs	24.6 hrs	24.6 hrs	24.9 hrs	43.5 hrs

Alien circadian rhythms operate on a forty-three-hour cycle, which would tend to indicate that they have evolved on a planet with a longer day-to-night period (i.e., a civil day of forty-three hours, midnight to midnight). Aliens sleep, on average, for sixteen hours per cycle.

24 hr rotation   43 hr rotation

IMMUNE SYSTEM

Laboratory trials have shown that aliens are immune to all known human viral pathogens, including smallpox, Ebola, HIV, pneumonia, and bubonic plague. This has not come as too much of a surprise to alien immunologists considering that cross-species infections are a relatively rare event in the nature world. But what has shocked medical scientists is their remarkable resistance to bacterial infections. Their bodies seem to have natural antibiotic properties. They show apparent immunity to such human banes as anthrax, cholera, botulism, leprosy, salmonella, and group A streptococcus. Needless to say, conventional biological warfare against aliens is futile.

As of yet, research scientists have been unable to extract and isolate the effective agents responsible for this resistance. The medical implications of this discovery could be profound for humanity.

Another interesting aspect of aliens' natural immunity to bacteria results in a resistance to the processes of decomposition. Alien corpses have been found effectively intact long after death.

Some have speculated that the new arrival of virulent diseases in recent years can be directly attributed to human-alien encounters. Others have gone further by suggesting that most of the contagious diseases that have plagued humanity throughout the ages have an alien origin. Yet, this position has little support among the majority of scientists working in the field. Authorities, however, are taking no chances. Aliens captured by the state are kept under strict quarantine conditions where there is little chance for cross-contamination. Due caution should always be exercised when handling living or dead aliens. Better safe than sorry.

ALIENS 102: PSYCHOLOGICAL CHARACTERISTICS

The intellectual ability of the alien mind is not questioned. Their highly advanced technologies are ample demonstration of their grand cerebral achievements. Alien brain-to-body size ratio is only slightly higher than our own. As larger brains generally equate to higher intelligence, it has been calculated that on a human IQ test, aliens would fall somewhere around the 140–160 mark. This, however, is only an assumption, as captive aliens have failed to cooperate in any form of psychological testing or intelligence profiling. Indeed, they have steadfastly refused to divulge any information at all about themselves to authorities, apart from their dietary preferences. What knowledge we have gained of their abilities has been solely through direct scientific observation.

Although alien intelligence may be higher than that of the average human, it does not surpass all human intellect. Many of our greatest intellectual luminaries would leave the average alien mind in the dark. Alien technologies have not arisen from their intellectual superiority, but from the advantage of having had a historical head start. No doubt, given the same amount of time, our species could develop comparable technologies. It must also be remembered that high intelligence does not always equate to common sense or "street savvy." Although it would be true to say that aliens currently

ESTIMATED IQ'S

Leonardo	Mozart	Einstein	Darwin	Alien
220	165	160	165	155

have the technological edge over us, the courage, ingenuity, and tenacity of the human spirit is still a force to be reckoned with. Aliens
can be outfoxed, outwitted, and outsmarted. Alien cunning, however, must never be underestimated. Many who have made this mistake have suffered the dire consequences.

EMOTIONS

The body language of aliens is notoriously difficult to read. Clinical
evidence has shown limited or no physiological reactions to normal
emotion-causing stimuli. Aliens do not display any of the emotional
states that we take for granted; compassion, joy, humor, anger, and
fear are not a part of their demonstrative repertoire. It remains unclear whether this is a result of their poor facial musculature or due,
rather, to the complete absence of these mental states.

One theory posits that they do have emotions, but rather than
being automatic nervous responses, these feelings are consciously
controlled. Emotions, as we can all attest, can interfere with our
ability to perform day-to-day tasks. Evolving the ability to switch
emotions on or off at will has provided aliens with a means of superior productivity, enabling them to move years ahead of us in the
development of their technologies.

Some have perceived the alien reaction of recoiling or running
away from danger as an expression of emotion. It is not clear, however, whether this is an expression of fear or just an automatic self-
preservation mechanism. The overwhelming evidence points to the
cold-hearted, calculating, dispassionate nature of our adversary.
Don't expect common courtesies.

PERSONALITY

To the untrained eye, aliens are physically indistinguishable from
one another. But with practice, you can recognize subtle variations

in facial features, body type, skin texture, and coloration. Numerous abductee anecdotes also indicate a distinct difference in the demeanor of individual aliens. Some accounts recall interrogation experiences reminiscent of the classic "good cop, bad cop" routine. Whether this is a revelation of individual character traits or just an expression of controlled emotion, we do not know.

The topic of alien personality has been hotly debated in recent years among academics. Do aliens have personalities, or are they no more than drones working in a hive? Can one alien be distinguished from another by their psychological characteristics alone? If aliens have personalities, how can we use this information to our tactical advantage? These questions will probably remain unanswered in the foreseeable future. It is enough to know that when you encounter an alien, you won't be assessing his potential as a golf buddy.

LANGUAGE

Aliens have a highly developed communication system, yet, in spite of the best efforts of linguists and technicians over the last half-century, their language remains, to this day, largely a mystery. Aliens do not "talk" in the sense that we speak. Aliens use a complex series of airborne electrical signals to silently communicate with each other. However, that is not to say that they are mute. Although the alien pharynx and vocal cords are much smaller and undeveloped by human standards, they are capable of making a range of vocalizations, ranging from shrill screams and high-pitch, almost inaudible, whistles to low purring sounds.

The greatest difficulty in translation is, of course, the fact that aliens communicate by a biologically generated electrical field. Laboratory analysis of these electrical signals has revealed an exceedingly complex form of communication. Although inaudible to humans, sound recordings reveal a high-frequency squeal and crackling noise similar to the sound of fingernails on a blackboard. Little progress has yet been made interpreting these signals. The difficulties faced in interpreting alien language could be compared with the challenges we face interpreting dolphin communications; we know they're saying something, but we just don't know what it is.

Under normal circumstances, aliens can "talk" to each other over a range of 40–50 yards. Communication over greater distances requires sophisticated transmission devices that have, on a number of occasions, been found surgically implanted within the heads of autopsied aliens.

Aliens are unable to communicate with each other if their electrogenic signals are blocked by some external barrier, such as the thick concrete walls in underground bunkers. Tests are still underway to determine the variety of substances that effectively block their transmissions.

Captive aliens have been taught rudimentary sign language in surprisingly short periods of time. They have readily communicated their immediate personal needs but have refused to provide any information relating to their origin or purpose here on Earth. Attempts at coercion using drugs and a wide variety of physical techniques have not met success. What they know, they're certainly not telling.

WRITTEN LANGUAGE

There is evidence to suggest that aliens use an advanced technology to directly record and then retransmit their electrogenically projected thoughts, bypassing the need for a written language. It is clear from inscriptions found on recovered alien artifacts, however, that they do continue to use a symbol-based language. This may be only a vestige of their linguistic history, in much the same way we continue to use Roman numerals for decorative reasons. As researchers have not, as yet, been able to interpret any form of alien language, the written symbols that represent the language remain a mystery.

SOCIAL STRUCTURE

Aliens display a simple social organization in which there appears to be no defined hierarchy. Each alien, although having different functions to perform, appears to have equal status within the group. Although quite capable of autonomous thought and actions, they function as a single coordinated unit, each knowing exactly what

the other is doing. (With this in mind, the phrase "take me to your leader" may not be an appropriate greeting during an initial encounter, as an individual leader may not exist.)

It is believed that a form of collective governance exists, where each alien, though acting as an individual, functions and makes group decisions as part of the larger whole, via the combined interconnective power of electrogenic communication. Working collectively, they can move as a single, seething organism, similar to a school of fish or flock of birds. This ability to "flock" has been used as a defensive mechanism when under attack. When flocking, aliens stay very close together and synchronized, avoiding collisions with each other, even when making sudden maneuvers. Changes in direction are carried out in unison by each member of the group at exactly the same moment.

It also appears that no single member of the group is greater than the whole. Aliens demonstrate an apparent willingness to abandon a fallen comrade if the safety of the group is in peril. That is not to say that they do not come to each other's assistance when in need. Aliens can sense the presence of other members of their species from a considerable distance and can home in on them without any visual references.

LEISURE

Researchers first began to explore the notion of alien recreation during idle moments in experimental research conducted on secret American Air Force bases during the 1950s. Attempts were made to engage aliens in a number of pursuits—including chess, football, poker, the yo-yo, and the hula hoop—all to no avail. After exhaustive trials, a number of academics concluded that all alien test subjects showed no inclination to participate in any form of human recreation. Whether this was indicative of a complete lack of interest on their part, an inability to comprehend the point of these diversions, or just a belligerent refusal to interact in any way, we do not know. Aliens isolated from one another in captivity seem to spend most of their "down time" in a state of torpor.

Nothing is known of alien recreation within their own society. Abductees testify that aliens seem to be obsessed with their work. But the same could be said if you were to observe doctors in a hospital emergency room or pilots landing a jumbo jet.

UNDERSTANDING THE ALIEN EARTH MISSION

There is substantial evidence to suggest that these denizens of deep space have been conducting their covert activities here on Earth for millennia. Both ancient legends and the earliest historical documents provide references to alien visitations. Extraterrestrial life forms have been known by many names, including angels, fairies, goblins, and bogeymen. They are so entrenched in our cultural psyche that their reality has drifted from our awareness.

Modern folklore has suggested that aliens come from any one of a number of star systems, including the currently popular Zeta Reticuli, a binary star system located about thirty-nine light-years from Earth in the constellation Reticulum. In reality, however, we know no more about where they come from than we do about how they got here. It is difficult to comprehend how it is possible to travel the vast distances of interstellar space within reasonable time frames. Any mention of wormholes, warp speeds, or transdimensional beings is pure speculation.

There is no doubt that we are part of a systematic study that has been going on for centuries. Why are they studying us? What would motivate their surreptitious investigations? We don't know.

THE ALIEN INVASION SURVIVAL HANDBOOK

FACT FILE # *197608BM-21*

FACT FILE NAME: *Repressed Memory Syndrome*

INCIDENT REPORT:

One of the long-term physical effects of alien abduction is the loss of memories associated with the ██████ abduction. Most people who have been abducted have no recollection of the event. Contrary to popular belief, abductees' memories are not "wiped clean" by the aliens; the memories are still there, but are inaccessible to the conscious mind.

Electroparalysis disrupts the storage of memories in the brain. Rather than being stored in the "conscious archive," by which we remember events in our day-to-day lives, it is stored in our "subconscious archive," which is only accessed under special ██████ retrieval conditions, such as regressive hypnotherapy.

The current popularity of this hypnotic technique among abductees is only matched by its lack of acceptance among the mainstream psychological profession, which maintains that hypnotherapy is highly unreliable, and that patients are open to suggestion and the creation of ██████ false memories.

It is difficult enough to speculate on what motivates humans to do the things they do. Don't, however, allow these questions to sidetrack you or make you hesitate. Ours is not to question why, ours is but to make them die.

From our own historical experience, we know that advanced human civilizations have often exploited less advanced civilizations—and species, for that matter. If we discover an ant nest in the backyard, do we try and communicate with them, ask them to take us to their leader, offer to share our technologies with them, or teach them about our world? No. We step on them. The clash of cultures and species usually results in bloodshed. Aliens have decided to study us, not to destroy us—at least, not yet.

THE RARITY OF ALIEN SIGHTINGS

Although it is unclear why aliens have visited Earth for so long without making meaningful contact, popular scientific opinion holds that either they are being prevented by some intergalactic protocol, such as a "prime directive," or making meaningful contact with our species is not priority for them. To put it simply, aliens don't want to be seen because they don't want their presence here on Earth undeniably confirmed. Sort of like God, in many ways. It is believed they operate under a principle of minimal interference, endeavoring not to disturb the natural development of human society. For the purposes of their studies, they can afford exposure to a small number of experimental subjects in the course of their day-to-day research, but this is a calculated risk. They effectively cover their tracks by "wiping" the memories of the majority of abductees. Those who do remember are considered delusional or attention seekers by the rest of society and are generally ostracized as loonies.

THE ALIEN INVASION SURVIVAL HANDBOOK

FACT FILE # *12018XR-07*

FACT FILE NAME: *Flying Saucers*

INCIDENT REPORT:

Although aliens have been with us for millennia, it wasn't until 1947 that their presence became widely publicized through an incident that captured the imagination of the world's media. On June 24 of that year, an aviation enthusiast named Kenneth Arnold, from Boise, Idaho, was piloting a CallAir A-2 on the return leg of a business trip when he made a brief detour to assist in the search for a missing ████████ military aircraft near Mount Rainier, Washington.

Around 3 p.m., while cruising at an altitude of 9,200 feet, he noticed a series of flashes in the sky. At first, fearing that he may have inadvertently flown into the path of another aircraft, he quickly scanned the sky around him, seeing only a distant DC-4 to the rear of his plane. Moments later, he saw the flashes again, this time pinpointing their location to the air space close to Mount Rainier, some twenty miles to the north. Eliminating reflections from aircraft windows and even a flock of geese as a source of the light, he watched as nine ████████████ objects flew in formation at a speed later estimated to be more than 1,700 miles an hour, faster than any known aircraft of the day. Arnold later stated that the "nine disc-shaped … objects were travelling incredibly fast. They were silvery and seemed to be

shaped like a pie plate." He said that they flew in a long
chain, "like the tail of a Chinese lantern," around mountain peaks and along valleys. Watching until they at last
disappeared from view in the distance, Arnold said that
they gave him an "eerie feeling," and he thought that
they must have been some sort of new top secret military
████████ technology.

After landing safely at Yakima, Washinton, he was
quick to inform airport authorities and friends of his
strange encounter. News of the incident traveled fast.
Bill Bequette, a reporter from the East Oregonian newspaper, interviewed Arnold for a feature article the following day, and is attributed by some as later coining the
phrase "flying saucer" after Arnold stated that the objects moved "like a saucer would if you skipped it across
the water." The incident was enthusiastically picked up
by newspapers and radio stations around the U.S. and then
internationally. The U.S. military denied having any
████████████ aircraft in the area at the time.

Arnold's testimony was corroborated by a number of
witnesses, including a United Airlines crew who, ten days
later, en route from Idaho to Washington state, saw between five and nine disc-shaped objects flying alongside
their plane for ten minutes before suddenly vanishing.

In the months that followed, thousands of "flying saucer" reports were filed around the world. It was only two
weeks after the Arnold incident that the most famous UFO
incident of that era occurred at Roswell, New Mexico.

HAVE YOU SEEN A UFO? HERE ARE SOME POINTS TO REMEMBER

1. You are not alone. You are not the first to have a close encounter with aliens, and you will certainly not be the last. There are many others having these same experiences on a daily basis around the world. Seek their support. Although at first it may be difficult to accept, the sooner you acknowledge the reality of your experience, the sooner you will be able to start preparing for your next encounter, which will come sooner than you probably expect.

2. It's only a matter of time. Statistics show that those people who see an alien spacecraft for the first time usually have a closer encounter within the next six to eight months. Multiple sightings within a short period of time is more than mere coincidence; it is a warning sign. You could very well be under surveillance and marked as a potential abductee. Now is the time to take precautions.

3. Take notes. Record the logistics of your encounter, including the time and date, and the spacecraft's direction of travel, estimated distance, size, and shape. Take a photograph, if possible. This data will help validate your claims when compared with other eyewitness testimonies.

4. Stay clear. When the aliens come for you, remember not to approach any grounded spacecraft. Close proximity may cause severe burns to exposed skin and result in recurring health problems. The primary danger periods are when the spacecraft's propulsion system is engaged: upon landing and when taking off. Three hundred feet is a safe distance.

UFO SPOTTING

When you spot an alien spacecraft for the first time, there is generally very little doubt about what you have just seen. Conventional explanations may momentarily flood your mind. Maybe it's just a strange cloud formation, a flock of birds, an aircraft, or a trick of the light. This, however, is just wishful thinking. As much as you may try to deny what you have just witnessed or rationalize it away, you have joined the ranks of those who know the truth of alien existence, and your world will never be the same again.

There are a number of distinctive characteristics that distinguish alien spacecraft from other aerial phenomena. Extraterrestrial spaceships come in a wide variety of shapes and sizes. Each type of craft is designed for a specific purpose. From discs to spheres, triangular landing craft to the vast alien mother ship, they are instantly recognizable as being not of this Earth. They can travel at speeds far greater than even the most advanced manmade aircraft. They are also highly maneuverable, having the unnerving ability to radically change their direction of travel within an instant, even at high velocities.

THE TRUTH ABOUT ABDUCTION

Alien abduction is a very real phenomenon that presents a clear and present threat to each and every one of us. Aliens can abduct anyone. They do not discriminate on the basis of geography, ethnicity, religion, age, economics, or politics. If you haven't been abducted yet, there is a good chance that you are already on their list.

The most vocal opponents to the existence of UFOs and extraterrestrials are generally those who have themselves been the victims of repeated abductions over many years. Covert government alien abduction researchers first noted this curious correlation during the late 1950s. They discovered that many abductees had not only undergone a form of brainwashing that resulted in a complete lack of memory of the events surrounding their abductions, but also a subsequent irrational denial of the very existence of their intergalactic tormentors. This strident, often shrill, opposition was noted in all sectors of society, from the heads of government and top scientists, to factory workers and high school janitors. Of more than six thousand individuals surveyed in North America alone, all were found to possess physical

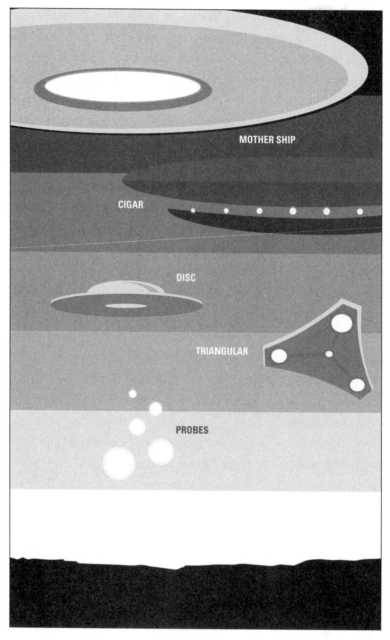

FIGURE 1.2: UFOs are reported in a variety of shapes and sizes.

signs of abduction, including implants, unexplained scars and incision marks, and anal bruising. Many now maintain that there is no greater confirmation of the alien menace than this widespread denial.

On the other end of the abduction spectrum, some misguided souls have gone as far as to suggest that they *want* to be abducted by aliens. Their feeling is that by doing so, they would prove once and for all the existence of aliens and alert all of humanity to their peril. Seeing is believing, in essence.

Bringing an abduction upon yourself is simply a matter of applying the George Costanza principle of doing the opposite of what you have been doing to achieve the opposite results. If what you have been doing has resulted in you not being abducted, then you must do the opposite. This would invariably draw their attention. Start visiting secluded backcountry roads, alone, late at night. Use your cell phone whenever possible to alert them to your location. Approach all strange-looking lights. Put yourself in situations conducive to an alien encounter, and they will come.

But remember, just because you can't remember being abducted doesn't mean that you haven't been already.

CHAPTER 2

DEFENSE

It is a doctrine of war not to assume the enemy will not come, but rather to rely on one's readiness to meet him; not to presume that he will not attack, but rather to make one's self invincible.

—Sun Tzu

CHAPTER SUMMARY

The key to defense from the nefarious schemes of our alien adversaries lies not only in knowledge of their vulnerabilities, but in the ability to utilize that knowledge to our advantage. Forewarned is forearmed. The best defense is always offense.

We live in a dangerous world. The very worst things that you can possibly imagine happen to people every day. Not because the people are bad or in any way deserve terrible things, but just because they are alive. Even getting up in the morning and going to work is fraught with untold dangers. Life is complex and dangerous enough without the ever-present threat of finding yourself naked, paralyzed, and being unceremoniously probed by aliens in a clinical examination room onboard an orbiting spacecraft. Whether you are at home, in the office, driving your car, or walking the dog, there are proven methods of protecting yourself, your loved ones, and your home from alien harassment.

PROTECTION FROM ALIEN PARALYSIS

Learning how to counteract alien mind-control techniques is the first step in protecting yourself and your loved ones from the ever-present threat of alien abduction. As explained in the previous chapter, aliens have the ability to paralyze humans by emitting an electrical impulse field from the frontal lobes of their brains. This has the effect of inhibiting human motor-neuron function, resulting in paralysis or the temporary lack of ability to move voluntary muscles.

In the following pages, we will reveal the hitherto unpublished results of secret research carried out by both private and government agencies over the last half-century. This research has proven conclusively that there are defense strategies to counter the aliens' primary weapon of control of our species.

REDUCE PROXIMITY

It has been well documented in both clinical tests and real-life case studies that alien electroparalysis is only effective over a limited range. Once outside that range, their attempts to paralyze you will be futile. This, in many ways, is similar to how your TV remote control works. Your remote control may be able to change channels when you're standing fifteen feet from your TV, but not when standing twenty feet away.

The range of an alien's electroparalysis field also depends on which direction the alien is facing. The field extends more than six feet in front of an alien, but only two feet behind. This is why many abductees have awoken in the night to find an alien squatting on their chest. It is also for this reason that a group of aliens, when under close-range attack, often form an outward-facing defensive circle, even when in retreat.

The effective range also varies depending on a number of other factors, including relative humidity and ambient air temperature, although their impact is minimal. This, however, is no more than a scientific curiosity and of no benefit to you outside of a laboratory situation.

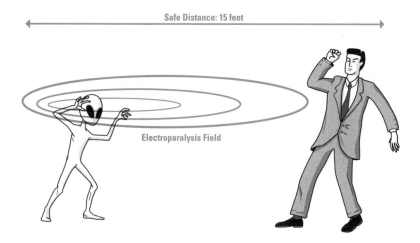

FIGURE 2.1: Remember to keep a 15-foot exclusion zone around all aliens until their electroparalysis field has been disabled.

As it is often difficult to judge distances in stressful situations, it is better to err on the side of caution and stay at least 5–6 yards away from an alien, or approximately the distance across a regular bedroom. Although it is always safer to approach an alien from the rear, do not forget that they can turn quickly, putting you within the danger zone.

DISARM THE SOURCE

Rendering the source of the electroparalysis field inoperable is also an effective way of thwarting an alien attack. As the field is generated within the alien's forehead, any number of techniques can be employed to disarm the source. The classic headshot from a long,

FIGURE 2.2: Use a classic headshot to disable alien electroparalysis fields.

medium, or short range, using any variety of weapons, is generally effective (see chapter 4).

Caution must always be shown when approaching aliens presumed dead or injured. Aliens have been known to feign injury and attack or paralyze people who approach too near.

AUDIO-PHONIC RESONANCE

The greatest tactical advantage aliens have over our species is their stealth, technological superiority, and ability to paralyze us, thus rendering us defenseless. All resistance must begin with overcoming the last and most insidious of these powers.

—Bluebird Report, 1996

Audio-Phonic Resonance (AR) is the term coined in the Bluebird Report to describe one of the electroparalysis-blocking techniques successfully employed by dozens of private citizens in attempted abduction situations. The common factor in many documented success stories is that potential abductees were listening to either music or some form of rhythmic chanting—real loud. This came as somewhat of a shock for all those involved in the research, and the correlation between music and survival is still repudiated by many scientists. How could music possibly provide an impenetrable barrier against alien attack?

Wilson and Curruthers's team undertook the arduous task of analyzing the full catalog of recorded music from 1877 to 1996. They discovered that not all types or styles of music or chanting were effective. From more than four million recordings, they found only ten that neutralized alien electroparalysis (see "The AR Top Ten," page 53). Researchers noted the fact that many of these songs are derived from the rock music tradition of the 1960s to the 1980s. Although they were able to determine that the effective recordings matched the resonance of a particular harmonic frequency that interrupts the electroparalysis effect on nerve endings in the human brain, further study was recommended.

The team also reported that, to be effective, music must be played at or above a critical threshold volume of 100 decibels. Live music worked just as well as recorded music; audiotapes, old 78 rpm records, CDs, and MP3 files were all equally effective, provided they were loud enough.

Although scientists do not fully understand how AR works, researchers are continuing with their efforts to determine the neurophysiological mechanisms responsible. Yet, not understanding how something works does not detract from its usefulness. (How many of us could explain how a microwave or a television works, for that matter?) Provided strict guidelines are followed, AR does work— offering an impenetrable barrier that gives the victim the opportunity to turn the table on his attackers and demonstrate that humanity will no longer be subjugated to their will.

How to Use Music to Thwart an Alien Paralysis Attack

1. ARM YOURSELF WITH A STURDY MP3 PLAYER. A lightweight, transportable audio device is an indispensable tool in your defense against the alien hordes. Nobody wants to find himself in an abduction situation only to discover that his MP3 player is just not up to the task. Choosing the correct device is an important decision. Your own personal security, and that of your loved ones, may depend on it.

2. MAKE SURE YOUR MP3 PLAYER IS APPROPRIATELY SHIELDED. The electromagnetic pulses created by UFO propulsion systems have been reported to cause a myriad of mechanical failures, instrument malfunctions, and electronic equipment disruptions. Electronic equipment can be protected from these surges by shielding them

THE ALIEN INVASION SURVIVAL HANDBOOK

FACT FILE # *0712VH-02*

FACT FILE NAME: *SETI*

INCIDENT REPORT:

How is it possible to search for signs of intelligent life on other worlds across the unfathomable distances of interstellar space? One way is to lift a metaphorical ear skyward and eavesdrop. In an approach similar to tuning your car radio to find local ███████ stations, scientists are, at this moment, scanning the skies in search of transmissions generated by advanced civilizations elsewhere in the universe. The Search for Extraterrestrial Intelligence (SETI) Institute (www.seti.org) is a private, non-profit ██████████ organization dedicated to the systematic search for intelligent ███████ alien life-forms. With billions upon billions of channels to scan, this is no easy task and has been likened to looking for the proverbial needle in a cosmic haystack. Although the program has now been running for more than forty years, there are still no signals that could be considered of intelligent origins—except for one anomalous beep, known as the "WOW!" signal, received on August 15, 1977, but the jury is still out on that one.

You can join SETI@home (http://setiathome.ssl.berkeley.edu) by downloading a free program that helps analyze raw radio telescope data ███████████ on your home computer. Who knows, you may be the one to lift the receiver and hear the first alien long distance call.

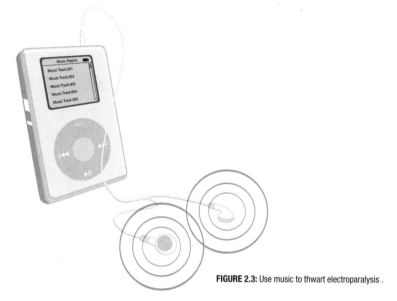

FIGURE 2.3: Use music to thwart electroparalysis .

in what is commonly known as a Faraday cage. This metallic enclosure consists of a conductive mesh that completely surrounds an
electronic device and prevents the entry of any electromagnetic field.
Faraday cages can be purchased commercially or custom made to
suit the design of your MP3 player. It is also recommended that
your shield be both waterproof and shockproof.

3. ENSURE THAT YOUR MP3 PLAYER'S BATTERY IS FULLY CHARGED. There are
few things worse than realizing you forgot to charge your MP3 player as aliens drag your paralyzed body toward their spacecraft. Play it
safe; charge this indispensable device at every opportunity.

4. CREATE A PLAYLIST COMPRISED OF THE AR TOP TEN. There are only ten
songs currently known to block alien electroparalysis. Others have
been found to be somewhat effective under laboratory conditions
but are, as yet, untested in real-life abduction situations. Authorities recommend that due caution be demonstrated when creating
an AR playlist. Only choose songs that have a 100 percent track
record of success.

5. SET THE SONGS TO LOOP. Most of the songs on the AR Top Ten list last for no more than five minutes. Although some abduction attempts last for less than five minutes, many have been protracted affairs lasting many hours. Aliens do not like to lose, particularly when a specific human subject is of significant importance to their nefarious studies.

6. TURN THE VOLUME UP TO THE MAXIMUM LEVEL. Research has shown that music played below 100 decibels has no effect on blocking electro-paralysis. As it is often difficult to determine the exact intensity of sound through earphones, it is best to play the music as loudly as your volume control will allow during an abduction attempt.

THE AR TOP TEN: TRACKS GUARANTEED TO BLOCK ALIEN MIND CONTROL

1. "Voodoo Child" by Jimi Hendrix
2. "Thunderstruck" by AC/DC
3. "My Sharona" by The Knack
4. "La Grange" by ZZ Top
5. "Helter Skelter" by The Beatles
6. "Get on Board, Lil' Children" by Shirley Temple
7. "Black Betty" by Spiderbait
8. "The Chicken Dance" by Werner Thomas
9. "Wild Thing" by The Troggs
10. any song performed by Tuvan throat singers

THINGS THAT WON'T PROTECT YOU FROM ALIEN MIND CONTROL

- Commercially produced or homemade helmets (e.g., tin foil)
- Cognitive resistance (e.g., rage, anger, indifference)
- A glass of water
- Prayers to a deity of your preference

How to Keep Your MP3 Player Safe During Combat Conditions

Extensive field trials of the Audio-Phonic Resonance technique have proven that while any one of the AR Top Ten is playing at 100 decibels or louder, you are invulnerable to alien electroparalysis. But in a combat situation, unforeseen circumstances may result in your MP3 player being damaged or otherwise rendered inoperative. Consider these basic precautions to ensure the music keeps playing and you remain safe from the grappling hands of your enemy.

1. TAPE YOUR EARPHONES TO YOUR HEAD. Duct taping your earphones to your head will ensure that they are not inadvertently pulled out during battle. It takes less than three seconds for an alien to paralyze you. The last thing you want is to be groping around in the dark looking for your earpiece and trying to fit it back into your ear while on the run.

2. SHORTEN YOUR EARPHONE LEADS. This will reduce the chances of them becoming snagged or ripped from your ears. Some advocates of duct taping even suggest taping the leads to your body to avoid snagging.

3. PLACE YOUR MP3 PLAYER IN A SECURE LOCATION. MP3 players are fragile devices and must be treated with care if they are not to fail at a critical moment. Protect your MP3 player from impact shocks, electromagnetic pulses, and water by placing it within a shielding device. Position the MP3 player high on your body with the controls always readily accessible.

4. PACK A "RESERVE." Having a spare MP3 player will ensure that if the worst happens, you will not be left to the mercy of your alien abductors. Keep it in a velcroed front pocket for easy access.

AUDIO-MORPHIC RECALL

Have you ever had a song trapped in your head, replaying over and over again, like a needle stuck in a record groove? This common phenomenon, known as Audio-Neuronal Looping (ANL), has tormented most of us at some point in our lives. Whether it lasts ten minutes or a week, it can consume our waking moments, driving us to the brink of insanity. ANL can be triggered by a single word or image. It is an entirely subconscious process that seems to come and go at random. These melodious obsessions have no known cure, except time.

The Bluebird Report states that in the absence of an MP3 player, the power of these tuneful cyclic annoyances can also be harnessed to thwart alien electroparalysis. This technique is called Audio-Morphic Recall (AMR). Numerous documented cases and laboratory tests have demonstrated that simply singing more than one of the AR Top Ten proves unsuccessful; however, by recalling one song from the list and "replaying" it in your mind continually, you can block alien attempts to paralyze you.

So how does it work? AMR is similar to singing along to your favorite song on the radio while driving at 80 miles per hour along a winding road in heavy traffic. Only yards from oncoming cars, you face almost certain death if you make even the slightest miscalculation. Yet, none of these details cross your mind as you are driving. It's as if you're on autopilot. You're doing what you have trained yourself to do, without even thinking about it. For AMR to be effective, it has to be an automatic response. The cyclical rhythm of your chosen song must throb away in your head no matter what bizarre events are happening around you. If you lose the tune for so much as a moment, aliens can regain control of your mind, rendering you helpless. Second attempts at escape are rarely successful.

THE ALIEN INVASION SURVIVAL HANDBOOK

FACT FILE # *071773HM-09*

FACT FILE NAME: *How to Listen In on Alien Broadcasts*

INCIDENT REPORT:

For decades, scientists have relentlessly searched for signs of intelligent ▮▮▮▮▮▮▮ life elsewhere in the universe. Programs such as SETI (Search for Extraterrestrial Intelligence) have, for more than half a century, unsuccessfully utilized highly sensitive radio telescopes to systematically survey the skies for radio transmissions from interstellar civilizations.

Unbeknownst to science, the very signals they have so fervently sought after have been here all along, under our very noses. You do not need millions of dollars worth of equipment or a Ph.D. in astrophysics to tune in to them. Your humble car radio or TV is capable of receiving extraterrestrial transmissions. These ▮▮▮▮▮▮▮ alien signals are commonly referred to as static, the electrical disturbance or hissing noise that is found between your radio or TV stations.

Static has long been attributed, in part, to cosmic microwave background radiation (CMB), which is the omnipresent form of electromagnetic radiation left over from the Big Bang. Recent studies have discovered that static holds a complex mathematical code cunningly concealed within what appears to be no more than a random electrical disturbance. This code has been deciphered using high-powered government computers to unveil prolific

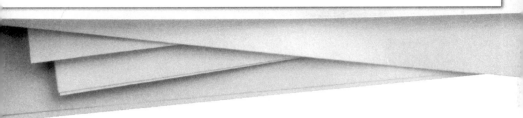

How to Condition Your Mind for Music Recollection

1. LISTEN TO THE MUSIC. This is the first and most essential step in building your defensive shield against alien electroparalysis. Even in the direst of circumstances, you must be able to rely on your memory. You cannot remember what you have not learned. The more you hear the songs, the more they will be indelibly etched into the neuronal pathways of your brain.

2. LEARN THE LYRICS. It is not enough to recall the tune and "dah-dah-dah" the words. Both melody and lyrics are symbiotically essential for the success of this technique. Commit them to memory.

3. PRACTICE, PRACTICE, PRACTICE. Try recalling your favorite songs under a variety of conditions—not just low-stress situations, such as taking a shower or driving the car, but during stressful or tedious ones such as an argument with your partner or waiting in an interminable line at the bank. If you cannot immediately recall a tune during a time of crisis, you are not ready to fend off an alien attack.

LOCATING AND REMOVING ALIEN IMPLANTS

Implants are rice-sized transmission devices surgically inserted in the bodies of human hosts during alien abductions. They are often metallic in composition and can be covered in a thin, organic membrane. They can be found anywhere on the body, from just under the skin, where they can sometimes be felt as a small, hard lump, or deep within muscle tissue or vital organs. Aliens have used implants to identify, track, and monitor human targets for centuries, but it has only been in recent years that their true purpose has been discovered.

Alien implants act as biotelemetry devices that monitor and record the human targets' basic physiological functions. They integrate themselves into the living tissue of their hosts and can survive undetected for decades. There is generally no pain associated with an implant. They come in a variety of shapes and can be found anywhere in the body, but they're always connected to the nervous system, providing direct access to the host's brain.

These extraterrestrial parasites also act as miniature global positioning systems, pinpointing the subject's precise geographical location. Although the method of transmission is still, largely, a mystery, it is thought that they somehow utilize the body's biochemical system to generate sufficient energy to operate as ultra-low frequency transceivers, effectively using the entire body as a mobile transmission tower.

Implants are usually in a state of dormancy, silently recording host data until activated by electromagnetic signals from an alien craft. The implant will then continue to transmit the host's data and position until it is switched off again.

Once removed from the body, implants no longer have a source of power and are immediately deactivated. They also seem to have a built-in self-destruction mechanism, causing them to undergo molecular breakdown within minutes of removal from living human tissue and rendering them useless for further scientific analysis. Attempts to reactivate implants by reinserting them into their original hosts or the bodies of surrogate hosts have proven ineffective.

Implants have been cunningly crafted to broadcast in a wide variety of typical human environments. However, a phenomenon similar to cell phone "drop out" can occur in dense urban areas where there are large concentrations of concrete and steel buildings,

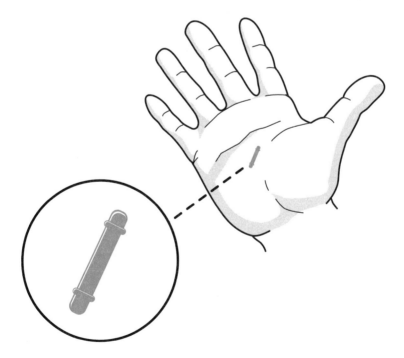

which block signals. This, of course, works to our advantage when we wish to conceal our location from our alien foes.

It is important to remember that there are few immediate, tell-tale signs that you have an alien implant. When you do have one, you won't "feel" any different. You won't set off shop checkout security alarms or start hearing radio broadcasts out of thin air. They are designed for long-term concealment and, in most cases, remain just that.

It is reasonable to assume that you have an implant if you have been abducted on one or more occasions. It is important that all implants (including decoy implants) are removed as soon as possible.

WHAT TO DO IF YOU HAVE AN ALIEN IMPLANT

1. DON'T PANIC. Unless aliens are in hot pursuit, there is generally no reason for immediate concern. Discovering an implant categorically proves that you have been abducted by aliens at some time in your life, and that you could again be taken at any time. Most people with alien implants have unknowingly had them for decades without any ill effect. Physiologically, they are no more dangerous than having a splinter. They should, however, be located and removed as soon as possible.

2. IF BEING PURSUED, SEEK IMMEDIATE SHELTER. Signals from alien implants are incapable of penetrating through more than a few feet of soil. This makes subways, disused mines, sewers, and any other such subterranean tunnel ideal for short-term or long-term shelter. The shielding effect of soil has been known for many years and has been used to great effect by a large number of people seeking immediate respite from alien harassment. The real threat of any subterranean environment comes not from pursuing aliens, but from the environment itself. Venturing into disused mines and cave systems

FIGURE 2.4: Seek underground shelter when evading pursuit by aliens.

should only be attempted by those with suitable speleological experience and equipment.

While hiding, remember:

- You can be pursued by aliens for at least 300 feet within an underground cavern.
- The deeper you hide, the better.
- The underground system you have entered should have more than one exit point. The aliens could be waiting for you when you come out.

3. ONCE YOU'RE IN A SECURE ENVIRONMENT, CONDUCT A THOROUGH SELF-EXAMINATION. Examine your body for any unexplained scars. Entry wounds are usually very small and discreet, or not visible at all. Implants are generally no larger than a grain of rice and come in shapes ranging from triangular to spherical. They can be located anywhere in the body. Subcutaneous implants are most readily identifiable, often felt as a small lump under the skin. Many people with these implants may mistake them for a deep splinter that they never remember getting. Skin surface implants are generally close to incision points. These incision points may, however, be virtually invisible. Stouthearted individuals in a tight situation may attempt removal of superficial implants with implements they may have at hand, such as a pocketknife or nail clippers. Remember to sterilize your equipment thoroughly before self-operation and dress the wound upon completion. Deeper implants will not be detectable by a casual examination.

4. IF AVAILABLE, USE A HANDHELD METER. A gaussmeter is a handheld device used for measuring the intensity of magnetic fields. When used to scan your body, it may indicate any electromagnetic disruptions, thereby defining areas for closer examination. Stud finders have also been used in the field on a number of occasions to locate a variety of superficial implants. Both these meters are available at hardware stores.

5. CONSULT YOUR RADIOLOGIST. Book yourself an appointment for a full-body X-ray at the first opportunity. Some implants are located deep within the body and cannot be found by a superficial examination. Many implants are discovered by accident when radiologists have been X-raying for unrelated reasons. Most hosts are unaware that they have an implant.

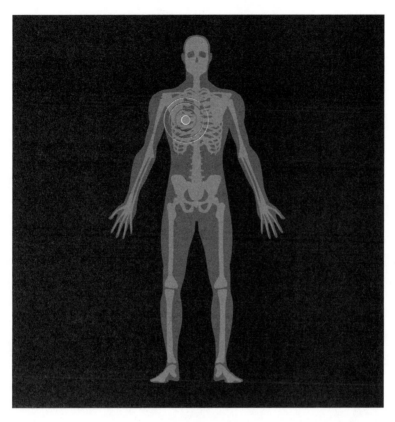

FIGURE 2.5: A routine X-ray may reveal hidden alien implants.

6. SEEK MEDICAL HELP. Deep implants require surgical removal and a local or general anesthetic. Surgical procedures should only be carried out by trained professionals.

7. SEND REMOVED IMPLANTS OFF FOR ANALYSIS. When removed, the implant may be covered with a sticky, gray, fibrous membrane. Do not remove this membrane. Have your surgeon place the implant in a sterile container and send it off for chemical analysis. You should find the results very interesting—that is, if government agencies ever allow you to see them.

DOMESTIC SECURITY: PROTECTING YOUR HOME

Once you have mastered the personal skills required to block alien mind control, you must consider the defense of your own home. Statistics reveal that a growing number of abductions occur from personal dwellings. You may wonder if it is indeed possible to protect yourself within your home from these interstellar intruders. The answer is yes ... to a degree.

Some are of the opinion that if aliens have traveled halfway across the galaxy to abduct us, then they are hardly likely to let a few bricks and a pane of glass stop them. This is not necessarily true. Contrary to popular mythology, aliens cannot materialize out of thin air in the middle of your living room. They cannot pass through walls or closed windows unscathed. You cannot be drawn up on a beam of light into their spacecraft. Aliens are bound by the same laws of physics that we are.

While at home, you have a tactical advantage: Nobody knows your home better than you do. All the necessary preparations can be made to preempt any incursion. Your home can be a place of refuge. Yet, your home need not be a fortress. A few simple precautions will greatly reduce the risk of waking up in the night with an alien squatting on your chest.

SECURING YOUR HOME

Although no home is absolutely secure from alien attack, there are some precautions that can reduce your vulnerability. These measures are not dissimilar to those recommended by police to protect your home from human intruders. Make sure you have:

- Deadlocks on all external doors
- Security bars on windows and doors

- A high perimeter fence surrounding your property
- Movement-activated external floodlights
- Guard dogs
- Tempered glass on all windows
- A backup power supply

Electromagnetic Sensors

In addition to the tactics mentioned above, the most effective domestic early warning system is a network of electromagnetic sensors placed at strategic locations around your property. These sensors register fluctuations in electromagnetic radiation levels associated with the close proximity of alien spacecraft. When triggered, alarms will provide you with sufficient time to prepare for an attack. Sometimes just the sound of an alarm will deter an alien attack. However, do not assume this to always be the case. At the sound of an alarm, you may have less than thirty seconds to prepare. Always err on the side of caution.

In many cases, household pets may sense fluctuations in electromagnetic levels before electronic sensors will. Do not ignore abnormal behavior. If your dog suddenly goes quiet or disappears after a frenzy of barking, you know it's time to swing into action.

Emergency Evacuation Plan

Although the safest course of action during an alien attack is to barricade yourself in your home, it may be necessary under some circumstances to evacuate the building as quickly as possible. Situations in which this would be advised include fire, dangerous electromagnetic radiation levels, and being overrun by superior numbers of invading extraterrestrials. It is important that each household member has a thorough knowledge of evacuation procedures, and spontaneous evacuation drills should be conducted on a regular basis. Your procedure should be as routine as taking out the trash. Delegate specific tasks to individual family members. Remember, when outside, you and your family are easy targets. Always demonstrate extreme caution.

In a successful emergency evacuation plan, it is important that each family member be aware of the following:

- Exit points, both primary and alternate
- Designated gathering point
- Evacuation routes, both interior and exterior
- Location of pre-packed survival kits
- Location and training in a range of weapons
- Techniques for deployment of decoys and booby traps
- Audio-Morphic defense principles

Home Audio System

Your home audio system need not be the top of the range, but it must be reliable, easy to access, and able to be heard from all parts of your home. Audio-Phonic Resonance defense systems rely on a volume of 100 decibels or more to be effective against alien electroparalysis. Make sure your home audio system is capable of sustained play at this minimum level of volume. Anything less and you risk being just another warm slab of meat on a cold operating table.

Ensure that you have the AR Top Ten (see page 53) either on standby or within easy reach of your hi-fi system. It is a good idea to practice loading and playing the CD in the dark. You should be able to load and arm your hi-fi system within ten seconds. Make sure you have a backup power supply and electromagnetic radiation shielding for extra security.

SURVEYING THE SCENE:
WARNING SIGNS AN ABDUCTION ATTEMPT IS IMMINENT

1. MISPLACED HOUSEHOLD ITEMS (ETA 2–3 WEEKS): Be alert if your TV remote control has been inexplicably moved, a pen has been mislaid, or only one sock returns from the washing machine. These could be signs of alien monitoring and surveillance; you could very well be on their abduction hit list. One or two isolated events should not be misconstrued as alien harassment, but disappearances on a regular basis cannot be ignored. Nothing is coincidental. Upgrade your security immediately.

2. PREMONITIONS (ETA 12–24 HOURS): If you've ever had a sense that someone is watching you, only to turn and see no one, you probably didn't look in the right direction—up. Don't believe those who say it's all just in your head. Your gut feeling is usually correct; someone is out to get you. Aliens have prospective victims under close surveillance for twenty-four to forty-eight hours prior to an abduction attempt. Be on high alert and implement your defensive action plan immediately.

3. UNUSUAL ANIMAL BEHAVIOR (ETA 15–20 MINUTES): Strange and erratic animal behavior prior to alien attacks has been observed in a wide variety of species, both domestic and wild, and is similar, in many respects, to unusual animal behavior before earthquakes. Anomalous behavior most often reported includes disorientation, fear, excitability, and frenzied vocalizations (e.g., barking)—or your pet simply heads for the hills. Animals have sensory abilities outside the range of human perception and are capable of detecting slight fluctuations in electromagnetic radiation caused by nearby alien spacecraft. Ignore these warnings at your peril.

4. ELECTRICAL INTERFERENCE (ETA: 5–10 MINUTES): Do not adjust your set. The interference on your TV may not be poor reception, but a sign of imminent home invasion. The close proximity of alien spacecraft has been known to produce electrical disturbances and power outages. The general rule of thumb is that the closer they are, the greater the disruption will be. Take any perturbations in electrical supply or TV and radio reception as a sign that you should prepare for immediate action.

5. THINGS THAT GO BUMP IN THE NIGHT (ETA: 1 MINUTE): Unexplained noises in your home could indicate that aliens have infiltrated your domestic security zone and are, at this very moment, creeping up your hallway toward your bedroom. Investigate all suspicious sounds, but remember to take the necessary precautions. Activate your audio system immediately and prepare for an attack.

6. PRESSURE ON YOUR CHEST AND COLD FINGERS AROUND YOUR NECK (ETA: NOW): When you awake from a deep sleep to find an alien squatting on

your chest with its hands around your throat, you can safely say that you've missed some of the early warning signs or failed to take appropriate evasive action. Being groped by an alien is not a pleasant experience. One abductee described it as feeling like large spiders crawling across her body. Alien body temperature is about 40°F (4°C) cooler than our own, and their hands feel somewhat clammy to the touch.

Don't panic. By the time you finish reading this manual, you will have all the knowledge and training you need to handle the situation. Read faster, and prepare to kick some alien butt.

URBAN DEFENSE:
PLAYING IT SAFE WHILE OUT AND ABOUT

The chance of being attacked by aliens increases by 76 percent the moment you step out your front door. It is not recommended that you isolate yourself from the rest of the world and adopt a siege mentality though. You must venture out in order to function as a productive member of society. Yet, it would be a mistake to think that just because you can't see aliens, they are not there. Here are some tips for improving your security while on the move.

Turn Off Your Cell Phone

Over the last twenty years, cell phones have developed from rare, bulky, and expensive pieces of equipment to mass-produced, low-cost personal consumer items. With more than 1.7 billion cell phones in the world, they have become a pervasive cultural phenomenon viewed as indispensable in today's technology-driven society.

It may come as a shock to many that recent studies conducted by the Lorenzo Institute in Milan have established a direct correlation between cell phone use and alien abduction.

Initially viewed by critics as merely coincidental, the rise in cell phone usage around the world has now been conclusively proven to parallel the dramatic increase in the number of alien abductions in recent years. It is estimated that cell phone use is growing globally at a rate of 40–50 percent per year, while abduction rates are increasing by a steady 35 percent per year. This research has also been used to help explain the imbalance that exists between abduction rates in developing nations and developed nations. As the personal use of cell phones increases in continents such as Africa and Asia, it is expected that we will witness a corresponding increase in alien activity. Statistical data has indicated that cell phone users are 345 times more likely to be abducted than non-cell phone users. Any use of your mobile phone, even just having it switched on in your pocket, may alert aliens to your exact location.

Consider that cell phones are no more than low-powered radio transceivers that use radio waves to transmit both oral com-

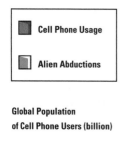

Global Population
of Cell Phone Users (billion)

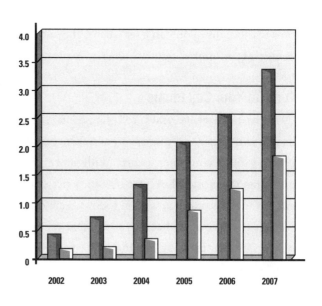

munication and data. Aliens are capable of tapping into these weak electromagnetic signals and to pinpoint your exact location anywhere on the face of the Earth. Even when you have no signal on your cell phone, it continues to emit radio waves that can be traced by aliens. Each phone carries its own unique signature code that allows aliens monitoring the airwaves to distin-

guish your phone from any other on the planet. Phones are such personal items that they are rarely far from their owners' sides, which effectively makes them alien navigation beacons.

Remember: The only safe cell phone is one that is switched off.

Strength in Numbers

The vast majority of alien abductions take place in areas away from human settlement, such as backcountry roads, national parklands, isolated homesteads, or remote rural locations. You can significantly reduce your chance of being abducted by remaining in population-dense zones, such as large cities or towns.

Alien modus operandi is stealth. They must do everything in their power to observe and monitor human activity undetected. Urban areas are generally avoided by aliens because they dramatically increase the possibility of mass human detection. If their existence and presence is verified by the general population of our planet, then they have violated their prime directive. Play it safe; stay in town.

Never Travel Alone

It is a well-established fact that you significantly increase the chance of being abducted if you are alone or in a very small group. Few people have been abducted while in a group of three or more people. Aliens find it easier to select and capture individual targets.

Although much of our lives are spent in major urban centers, it is sometimes necessary to venture into the countryside. If you must travel through isolated areas, it is essential that you never travel alone. Make sure that you have as many companions with you as possible; two other people are an absolute minimum. Never split up. If you are separated, it is far easier for the aliens to pick you off one by one.

The techniques of Audio-Phonic Resonance and Audio-Morphic Recall are also more effective in group situations. If one of your group members loses concentration or there is a mechanical problem with his or her MP3 player, you have some backup. Other members of your team can launch a counterattack and drag you away to a safe location.

Avoid High UFO-Traffic Areas

Restrict your travel through areas where UFOs have recently been active. Aliens tend to focus their attention on particular regions over a period of time. Monitor the radio and the Internet to stay up-to-date with regional developments and information on alien activity along your proposed route.

Only Travel During Daylight

Most UFO sightings and abductions occur at night. If you must travel alone or in a small group in isolated areas, you can significantly reduce the possibility of being abducted by making essential travel only during daylight hours. As more humans are active during the daytime, aliens reduce the possibility of detection by conducting most of their activities during the hours of darkness. That is not to say, however, that they are exclusively nocturnal. Their studies draw them out during daylight hours when the rewards justify the increased exposure.

ON THE ROAD

Some of the most famous abductions have occurred while people have been traveling by automobile—Betty and Barney Hill, Travis Walton, Herbert Schirmer, to name but a few. As many of us find ourselves sitting behind the wheel for many hours each week, it is important to consider some of the implications relating to our defense from alien stalkers while on the roads.

HOW TO AVOID ABDUCTION WHILE DRIVING

1. DRIVE IN CONVOY. Driving in isolated locations increases the risk of abduction. You can reduce the danger by always driving in a convoy of at least two or three other cars. Make sure that all members of your party are thoroughly trained and kitted out for your trip. You don't want to have to engage in unplanned rescue attempts of untrained people, thereby endangering yourself and the rest of your party.

2. TURN OFF YOUR CELL PHONE. Don't assist aliens by broadcasting your position via a cell phone. Turn it off while in transit.

3. AVOID TRAVEL AT NIGHT. It has been statistically proven that the majority of alien attacks occur after nightfall. Reduce your chances of a surprise abduction attempt by only traveling during daylight. If you must travel after dark, make sure you travel in convoy.

THE ALIEN INVASION SURVIVAL HANDBOOK

FACT FILE # *1673zXR-04*

FACT FILE NAME: *The Betty and Barney Hill Incident*

INCIDENT REPORT:

The modern era of widely publicized alien ▮▮▮▮▮ abductions began with what's now commonly known as the Hill Abduction. On the evening of September 19, 1961, Betty and Barney Hill were driving home when, just south of Groveton, New Hampshire, they saw what they initially thought was a shooting star.

When they stopped to investigate, they observed a large alien craft descend within yards of their vehicle. Through windows in the ▮▮▮▮▮▮▮▮ craft, Mr. Hill could see humanoid figures operating a variety of instruments. Frightened, the Hills drove away at a high speed, only to experience an inexplicable series of mechanical problems and beeping sounds from the rear of their car.

After later reporting the incident to the U.S. Air Force and experiencing a number of recurring nightmares, the Hills realized that they had, in fact, been abducted by aliens. Subsequent hypnotherapy unlocked their repressed memories, revealing that they had been taken onto the ▮▮▮▮▮ spacecraft and subjected to a range of experiments. This phenomenon of "missing time" is common among alien abductees, and explains why most are unaware of their abduction experiences. The Hill incident made front-page news and went on to encourage many more abductees to come forward and reveal their own stories.

4. TAKE EVASIVE ACTION. If an alien spacecraft is sighted, head immediately toward an area of higher population density. Remember, the chances of being abducted reduce when you surround yourself with more people. If in an isolated area, drive to a roadhouse or farmhouse. Hide under bridges or in tunnels for immediate shelter. It is impossible to outrun an alien spacecraft, and it is dangerous to try.

5. UPGRADE YOUR CAR AUDIO SYSTEM. Install the best car audio system your money can buy. Make sure that it is encased with a Faraday cage to protect it from electromagnetic radiation surges. Remember, volume is of critical importance when creating an Audio-Phonic shield.

6. EQUIP YOUR RIDE WITH THE AR TOP TEN. The importance of the counter-abduction AR Top Ten cannot be overstated. It is imperative that you have a personal copy on hand at all times, both in your CD player and in an MP3 player, and that you also have the songs committed to memory as a backup strategy in case your sound system goes down.

7. PAY ATTENTION TO SPONTANEOUS MECHANICAL PROBLEMS. If your car unexpectedly stalls and your lights go out while driving through a remote area at night, you know that you're in for trouble. Lock and load, and prepare for an imminent abduction attempt. Don't panic. You know what to expect, and you're ready for it. You are now in automatic mode. If your car's audio system fails, get out of your car and head for the nearest shelter. Leave your headlights switched to the on position so that when the danger has passed, they will come back on, alerting you that it's now safe to return to your vehicle.

IN THE WILD: PROTECTING YOURSELF WITH THE USE OF TRAPS

Aliens are some of the most difficult creatures to successfully defend against in the wilderness. With limited resources at your disposal, you are completely reliant on your own personal adaptability and ingenuity to protect yourself and your loved ones from their malevolent intentions. Although they have the technological advantage, it is possible for people using primitive tools and materials to trap, capture, or kill unsuspecting hostile aliens. Alien traps have been used with great effect under the most challenging of circumstances and can provide a formidable defensive barrier between you and your adversaries. Traps may also have the effect of demoralizing your foe to the extent that they may decide you are not worth the trouble and go and find easier prey.

Before looking at a variety of alien traps, it is important that we examine some general rules.

BEST PRACTICES FOR ALIEN TRAPS

1. THE TRAP YOU CHOOSE MUST BE A PERFECT MATCH. A trap must suit the location in which it is constructed. Pay attention to detail. Ensure that the materials from which the trap is constructed are from the immediate vicinity so that it will blend in to the local environment.

2. KEEP YOUR TRAP SITE PRISTINE. Make sure the trap site is altered as little as possible. Nothing must be out of place. Dead grass, withered branches, and freshly dug or trampled soil all indicate something is amuck. Leave nothing to indicate recent activity. Construct your trap devices away from the area in which you intend to set them. This will minimize the visual disturbance to the trap area.

3. ALWAYS CAMOUFLAGE. As traps usually utilize wire, rope, or a trip stick as part of their trigger mechanisms, these must be carefully concealed to prevent detection. Use leaves, grass, soil, mud, or water to cover these telltale signs of human activity.

4. BE MINDFUL OF YOUR TRIGGER. The trigger device must be simple, weather-resistant, easily hidden, and made from local materials. Of the diverse range of trigger devices that can be used, the "figure four" trigger (illustrated at right) is probably the simplest and one of the most reliable.

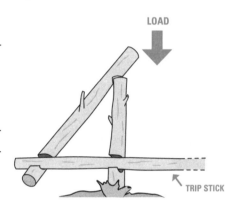

LOAD

TRIP STICK

TYPES OF ALIEN TRAPS

Alien trapping involves the construction of a mechanisms that, when triggered, will either kill or maim your prey. They must be simply designed, easy to construct, and foolproof. There are two basic forms of traps:

- **BOOBY TRAPS:** Booby traps utilize a range of technologies that require expert training and handling, including explosives and chemical and incendiary devices. Although these devices are all part of the modern tools of war and are very efficient, they are not for the novice alien fighter.

- **PRIMITIVE TRAPS:** Primitive traps are constructed from resources readily available in any wilderness location from tools that you may have at hand in a survival situation, including a knife, ax, shovel, wire, or rope.

For the purposes of this book, we shall assume that you do not have complex military items at your disposal and must rely solely on available resources. Primitive traps come in a variety of forms. The type of trap you choose will depend on a number of factors, including the nature of the terrain you find yourself in, the time and resources you have available, the manpower you have at your disposal, and the desired outcome. Choosing the correct trap for the situation you find yourself in will, to a large degree, determine how effective it will be. In this section, we will look at a number of classic primitive alien traps that have been successfully used in real-life situations.

A note of caution: All the traps described in this book do work and are extremely dangerous. The construction of traps should be attempted only under the direst of circumstances and never in populated areas.

Classic Pit Trap

Preparation time: 6–8 hours

Level of difficulty: medium

Location: woodland or forest

A pit trap is a large hole dug into the ground and concealed in such a way that an un-suspecting alien will fall in and impale itself on a series of sharpened stakes at the bottom. Together with traditional snare traps (a simple trap constructed from a coil of rope or wire concealed along a path that, when triggered, hoists the unsuspecting victim by the ankle skyward, to be left dangling upside down from a tree limb), the pit trap is often the first that people think of when traps come to mind. Building an effective pit trap takes a considerable amount of time and effort. It is not the type of trap that can be set in haste and, as such, is generally more suited to defending well-established positions where you have dug in for the long haul. It should not be attempted by those in a hurry or those with insufficient manpower. Here are the steps for effective pit-trap construction:

1. POSITION: As with all alien traps, positioning is of critical importance. Optimally, traps should be constructed along seldom-used trails or paths. A detour around an obstacle such as a fallen tree or a large puddle on the main path is an ideal location. These obstacles will funnel your prey to where you want them. The immediate presence of thick, trampled undergrowth is a distinct advantage when it comes to camouflage.

2. CHECK BEFORE YOU DIG: You can save yourself a lot of time and effort by ensuring that the soil type is satisfactory before you start. Reject water-logged or sandy locations, as these will require substantial reinforcing to the internal walls to prevent collapse. Make sure there are not too many large rocks or roots that will impede your progress.

3. PIT CONSTRUCTION: The pit should be about nine feet deep. Remove all soil at least 50 yards from the pit site, being careful to avoid trampling surrounding vegetation. It is vitally important that you do not leave any evidence of freshly dug soil around the site. Plastic or canvas sheets may be used to protect the immediate vicinity from undue soiling during construction. If necessary, brace the sides of the pit with local timbers.

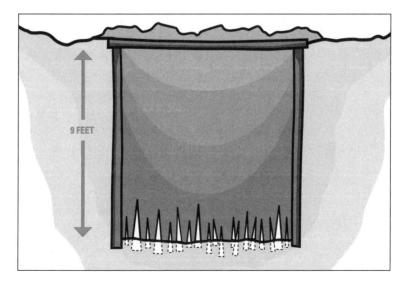

9 FEET

FIGURE 2.6 A: Typical pit trap construction.

4. STAKE YOUR CLAIM: Although your interstellar adversary may be injured by merely falling into your pit, other measures must be taken to effectively detain it. Cut fifty or sixty spikes (2–3 feet in length) from local timbers, trimming one end to a sharp point. Embed the spikes vertically into the bottom of the pit, pointy side up. Ouch! That's got to hurt.

FIGURE 2.6 B: Proper spike carving technique.

5. CONCEALMENT: The entrance to the pit must be covered in such a way that it will remain securely in place until your enemy steps on it. It must then readily give way, allowing your victim to fall onto the spikes. Construct a light timber frame to cover the top of the pit. Cover this frame with vegetation or soil from the immediate area. When complete, it should be indistinguishable from its surroundings. Use light internal bracing, if necessary, to support the roof of the trap.

FIGURE 2.6 C: Concealment is the key to pit trap success.

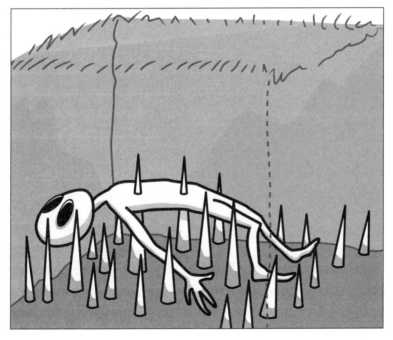

FIGURE 2.6 D: Victory is yours.

Peruvian Rockfall Trap

Preparation time: 3–4 hours

Level of difficulty: medium

Location: mountainous terrain with abundant rocks

If you find yourself in a mountainous environment when being pursued by aliens, the Peruvian rockfall trap has the advantage of being both relatively easy to construct and conceal. This trap unleashes a cascade of boulders on your hapless prey, sweeping them into oblivion.

The three basic requirements for this trap are a ready supply of large rocks, a slope of sufficient gradient for them to roll down, and at least 100 yards of heavy-grade wire for the trip mechanism. Here's how to build the trap:

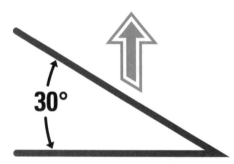

1. POSITION: Select a steep, exposed slope (the gradient must be greater than 30°), free of any natural features, such as trees or large rocks that the hapless aliens could shelter behind.

2. PLATFORM CONSTRUCTION: Select a position at least 100 yards uphill from the target zone, and build a sturdy log platform propped up by suitable supports. Ensure that these vertical supports are carefully balanced on a rounded log, so as to easily pull free when triggered from below. Collect boulders (at least fifty pounds each) and roll or drag them on top of the platform. If possible, get help with heavy rocks, and always keep your back straight when lifting. Multiple traps can be made along a slope to increase the chances of a successful hit.

3. TRIGGER DEVICE: Balance a boulder on the outside of the path directly below the platform in the target zone. Inconspicuously run a wire from the platform supports to the path and tie it to the boulder, providing enough slack to allow the boulder to gather

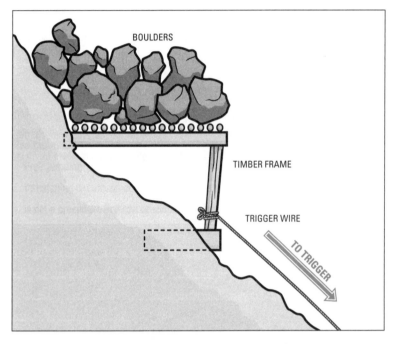

BOULDERS

TIMBER FRAME

TRIGGER WIRE

TO TRIGGER

FIGURE 2.7 A: Platform construction

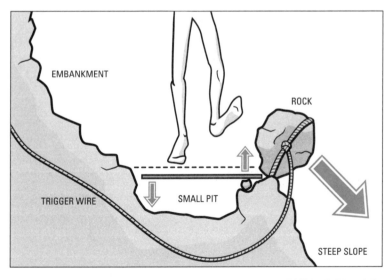

EMBANKMENT

ROCK

TRIGGER WIRE

SMALL PIT

STEEP SLOPE

FIGURE 2.7 B: Trigger device

sufficient speed before snapping the wire tight. Dig a shallow hole on the path adjacent to the boulder. Insert a sturdy stick or two under the boulder, supported on a fulcrum (e.g., a small rock) and projecting out into the hole, level with the path to act as a lever when stepped on.

4. CONCEALMENT: Camouflage the top of the hole with local materials. When an alien steps on the trigger sticks, the boulder will be levered off the edge of the slope, causing it to pull out the supports of the platform and unleash a tsunami of boulders down upon the alien.

> **NOTE:** It is possible to construct a series of platforms holding thousands of pounds of rocks. Once triggered, one rockslide would trigger another, creating a potential rockfall zone of hundreds of yards. This would alleviate any possibility of an alien escaping the target zone prior to the rocks reaching it.

Vlad the Impaler Trap

Preparation time: 1–2 hours
Level of difficulty: medium
Location: woodland or forest

This trap derives it name from the fifteenth-century Romanian prince who systematically impaled his captives on stakes. It involves suspending a sharpened stake or log in the treetops that, when triggered, swings down and impales its unsuspecting alien victim. Setting the trap often requires a lot of fine-tuning to achieve perfect balance and delivery of the log. When selecting a location, look for a light to medium understory and sufficient foliage in the canopy to conceal the suspended stake. Here are the steps for proper trap construction:

1. CHOOSE A STAKE: Select a straight, sturdy ten-foot (6–12 inches in diameter) branch. Sharpen both ends to a point. Remove any offshoots or leaves that may snag on surrounding foliage.

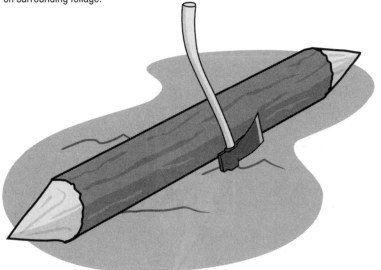

FIGURE 2.8 A: Choose a lengthy branch for your stake.

2. POSITION: Choose a narrow path with little room to maneuver on either side. Suspend the stake from a limb (12–15 feet above the ground) of a sturdy tree. When hanging, the stake should be resting at waist height. Pull the stake up to an angle just short of 90°.

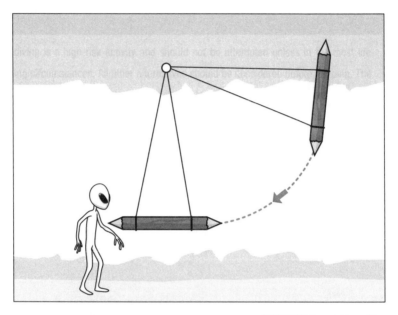

FIGURE 2.8 B: Correct stake position.

3. TRIGGER DEVICE: Use local materials to camouflage the trip stick, rope, and stake. Once set, avoid walking within the drop zone.

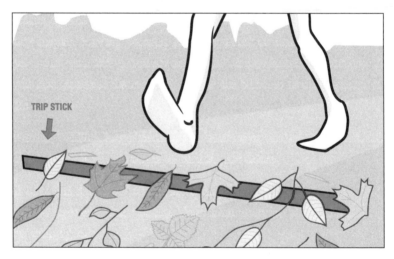

FIGURE 2.8 C: Employ an approprate trigger device.

The Porcupine Trap

Preparation time: 1–2 hours
Level of difficulty: easy
Location: woodland or forest

The porcupine trap is similar to Vlad the Impaler in that it utilizes a log hoisted into the treetops, but it varies in that the log drops vertically onto the unsuspecting alien rather than swinging down.

This trap is particularly suited to woodland and forest environments with sufficient canopy cover to conceal the spiked log. Ensure a section of path is selected with dense understory on either side, so as to reduce the chances of your prey diving to one side when the trap is triggered. Here are the trap instructions:

1. LOG SELECTION: Choose the heaviest log that: (1) you are capable of lifting without personal injury, and (2) is capable of being supported by the ropes you have available. Embed 10-inch spikes at 12-inch intervals across the surface of the log.

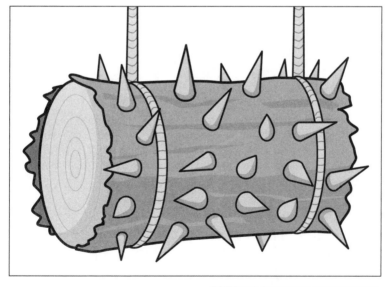

FIGURE 2.9 A: Select a heavy, yet manageable log.

2. POSITION: Hoist the log into the canopy, being careful to avoid entangling the spikes in the surrounding foliage. Thin guy wires may be used to reduce movement from the wind or rope twists. These should easily pull free as the log drops. The log should run parallel to the trail beneath. Avoid walking under the log when in position.

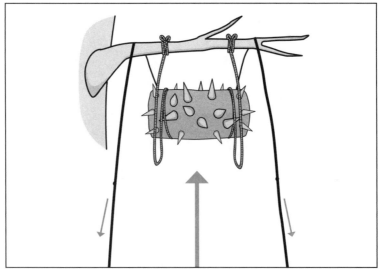

FIGURE 2.9 B & C: Correct porcupine trap positioning.

3. CAMOUFLAGE: Camouflage your trap and its trigger using local materials. Ensure these materials will not snag or catch on the log as it drops, or create a noise that will warn your prey of their impending demise.

Traps are not deterrents built in haste. They take time, effort, and resources to construct.

They are most suited for siege situations or when you're on the run and want enough security to ensure a good night's sleep. They are, by their very nature, defensive.

However, there comes a time when defense is just not enough. You may reach a point where all the precautions you have taken are insufficient to get you out of a sticky situation, and you'll need to employ other tactics.

CHAPTER 3

ESCAPE

> He that fights and runs away, may turn and fight another day: but he that is in battle slain, will never rise to fight again.
>
> —Tacitus

CHAPTER SUMMARY

No matter how thorough your anti-abduction training is, there may come a time when, in an unguarded moment, you succumb to the malicious intentions of our alien foes. If you are captured, like countless others around the globe, do not despair. Escape is possible.

If all the preventive measures outlined in this book have been strict-
ly followed, you can be 97 percent sure you are safe from alien abduction. That only leaves 3 percent to worry about.

What if things don't go according to plan? In the confusion of
your first close encounter, you forget the lyrics to "Voodoo Child."
The battery in your iPod goes flat. You are abducted while asleep,
or you are unexpectedly overpowered by a seething mass of our interstellar adversaries. Any one of a hundred unforeseen events can
thwart even the most thorough counter-abduction training. Must
you abandon hope? Definitely not. Escape is not only possible, it
has been achieved by a surprisingly large number of ordinary people under a wide range of extraordinary circumstances.

Escape, however, is a venture that should never be taken lightly. Fleeing from your alien abductors is a serious undertaking fraught with a unique set of challenges and unforeseen dangers. Yet, when weighed against the perils of remaining captive, escape, no matter how dangerous, is the only real alternative left to those who do not wish to subject themselves to the indignities of a lifetime of harassment and experimentation.

In addition to physical stamina, a successful escape will require courage and cunning, but also a considerable amount of good luck. Yet, the key ingredient in any escape situation is always the mental attitude of the person involved. Being proficient in the necessary skills is important, but having the will to survive is essential.

ESCAPING FROM YOUR ALIEN CAPTORS

Although the circumstances of abductions may be unique, there are some general rules that can be followed.

1. REMAIN CALM AND FOCUSED. It is vital that you don't panic. You have a job to do, and it will take all of your concentration and determination to succeed. Like any strange and new environment, alien spacecrafts hold much to distract you from your primary objective. The novelty of your extraterrestrial surrounding, peculiar sounds and smells, and the unnerving sensation of gangly fingers probing every inch of your body can all divert your attention from your task. Take a deep breath, relax, think—then act.

2. PLAN AN EARLY ESCAPE. Seventy-three percent of all successful escapes occur within the first thirty minutes of captivity. It is during this period that you are still capable of functioning at your peak; the longer you remain under alien control, the more your physical ability and mental resolve to escape will be impaired. So, start planning your escape and watching for opportunities the moment you are captured.

3. BE OBSERVANT. Pay attention to your surroundings. Take note of the route you take within the spacecraft, watching carefully for reference points that will help you retrace your path back out of the ship. Also look for any side corridors, ventilation shafts, or other alternative exit points. Are there any items that could be used to aid your escape or to use as a weapon? Note the location and number of aliens along your route. Even small things, which may initially seem insignificant, could be of vital importance later on.

4. ACT IMMEDIATELY. The saying "he who hesitates is lost" is never truer than when attempting to escape from your alien abductors. When an opportunity to escape presents itself, it is imperative that you act immediately, as you may not get a second chance. Be prepared to adapt your strategy to suit the situation, which may change from moment to moment. Watch and wait. If you notice the aliens are distracted or momentarily let down their guard, you must be prepared to act instantly. Chances to escape have been lost by those waiting for just the right circumstances. There is no time like the present. Do it now.

5. ROCK ON. The very fact that you have been captured and are onboard an alien spacecraft indicates that you were probably without a functional or adequately shielded MP3 player (refer to chapter 2). Any successful escape attempt will hinge on your ability to employ the Audio-Morphic Recall techniques discussed in the previous chapter. Some have likened the difficulty of this level of concentration to reciting Shakespeare's "Cry 'God for Harry, England, and Saint George!'" speech from *Henry V* ("Once more unto the breach, dear friends ... ") while running in front of a herd of stampeding wildebeests. While it is true to say that this may seem like an impossible task, it is one that must be mastered if you wish to thwart your adversary's intentions. You can gain comfort from the knowledge that other ordinary people from many different cultures and walks of life have successfully used this technique under a diverse range of circumstances to aid their escape.

6. REMEMBER THAT THE MEEK WILL NOT INHERIT THE EARTH. Aliens rely on our total submission. Their whole strategy is based on their ability to subdue us, then—and only then—to exploit us. Compliance with your captors may get you home again, but not undamaged, or un-scarred, and with the certain knowledge that you will be abducted again. If you are to oppose your captors, you must do so forcefully and in such a way that they will decide that you are not worth the trouble and will go elsewhere to find more cooperative victims.

History has demonstrated that bravado can be effectively em-ployed to provide a tactical advantage. Berserkers were ancient Norse warriors legendary for working themselves into frenzy be-fore a battle and then fighting with reckless savagery. The mere thought of them was sufficient to send some enemies running for the hills. In the same way, you must demonstrate to your abductors that you will not go quietly, like a lamb to the slaughter.

When faced with a bull in a china shop, the most prudent course of action is to open a door to let it out. In the same sense, when your alien abductors are confronted with a human specimen that cannot be subdued by mind control and is on the rampage within the confines of their spacecraft, they will do whatever it takes to get you out of their ship as quickly as possible.

Having gone to all that trouble to abduct you in the first place, aliens are not likely to want you dead if they can at all avoid it. Your corpse is of little use to their experiments, which all seem to target life processes. In addition, letting you go, if things start to

THREE STRATEGIES FOR UNLEASHING HELL ONBOARD AN ALIEN SPACECRAFT

The best course of action is physical aggression. To put it bluntly, take out as many aliens as possible. Having turned the tables on your captors, now turn their heads, literally, until they snap off. Leave them with no doubt that you mean them harm and you do not, in any sense of the word, come in peace.

Feel free to engage in wanton destruction; vandalize anything you can get your hands on. Aliens are a long way from home, and the last thing they want is to have their life-support systems damaged. Demonstrate that the risk of keeping you onboard far outweighs any benefits.

And finally, feign insanity. Scream like a banshee, wail and roar, whatever it takes. Don't hold back. Remember, aliens can only hear high-pitched sounds. There is nothing more fearful than being locked in a confined space with a creature that is out of control and apparently has no concern for its own safety. Anything can happen, and usually does.

get rough, provides them with the option of recapturing you later when they are better prepared. But be warned, accidents can and do happen. Death through misadventure during escape attempts is not uncommon. Due caution must always be demonstrated.

To date, aliens have revealed to those who've been abducted only one real weapon in their armory: mind control. They have used this formidable power to their advantage, unchallenged, throughout their entire association with mankind. When this power is overcome, they are rendered effectively defenseless.

A combative and maliciously destructive human is a threat to not only their own personal safety, but to the security of their ship. Professor A.C. Bishop, working with case studies during a clandestine military research project near Havelock, North Carolina, in the late 1980s, identified three behaviors, which, if applied with appropriate vigor and enthusiasm, will almost guarantee prompt eviction from any alien spacecraft.

7. ABANDON CAUTION. Trying to avoid detection while onboard an alien spacecraft is futile. Elaborate biomonitoring systems are able to instantly pinpoint your location and track every move you make. There is little point trying to sneak down corridors or hide in dark recesses. Abandon all pretenses of stealth and head toward your goal without hesitation or restraint. Success will not be achieved by the cautious.

8. TAKE NOTHING BUT MEMORIES (LEAVE NOTHING BUT CORPSES). Resist the temptation to take any mementos from the spacecraft upon your exit. Although you may think they would look good on your mantle or prove themselves useful for verifying your story to the media, most escapees who have souvenired any unsecured items have soon been recaptured.

THE ALIEN INVASION SURVIVAL HANDBOOK

FACT FILE # *730730MS-22*

FACT FILE NAME: *The Valentich Disappearance*

INCIDENT REPORT:

On October 21, 1978, a twenty-year-old pilot named Frederick Valentich disappeared while flying a small Cessna over Bass Strait, Australia. The incident received huge media attention at the time and remains to this day one of the most widely publicized ████████ mysteries in Australian aviation history.

Valentich was on a routine, one-hour flight between Moorabbin Airfield and King Island when he radioed Melbourne air traffic control that he was being buzzed by a large ████████████ object that was "not an aircraft." He said, "It seems to me that he's playing some sort of game; he's flying over me two, three times at speeds I could not identify." He described it as fast-moving and having "a long shape." He said, "The thing is just orbiting on top of me; also, it's got a green light and it's sort of metallic, like it's all shiny on the outside." Moments later, his last ████████████ transmission was " ... that strange aircraft is hovering on top of me again. It is hovering, and it is not an aircraft." What followed was a loud, metallic, rasping sound for seventeen seconds, then silence. An intensive air and sea search found no trace of the pilot or plane.

Alien artifacts are engineered from extraterrestrial alloys that are readily traceable. Onboard remote sensing instrumentation can home in on stolen equipment from many miles away. Even a small surgical tool can act like a beacon, broadcasting your location. If you use any alien equipment as a weapon while escaping, make sure that you dispose of it within the first 300 feet of the craft, unless, or course, you propose to use it as a lure or a decoy to throw them off your trail.

ESCAPE SCENARIOS

ESCAPE SCENARIO	GENERAL CHARACTERISTICS	% OF ESCAPES
LEVEL I Pre-Boarding	Escapes that occur during an attempted abduction. These escapes occur before being taken into an alien craft. Escapes typically occur while the potential abductee is still in his or her own home, another dwelling, or in an exterior urban or rural/wilderness landscape.	68
LEVEL II On the Ground	Escapes that occur after being forcibly taken onboard an alien craft that has not yet become airborne. The abductee escapes out of the craft at ground level.	30
LEVEL III In the Air	Escapes that occur from an alien craft while in flight within the atmosphere. Involves leaping from the craft while in motion either into water or onto land. Extremely hazardous. High injury/death rate.	2
LEVEL IV In Space	Escapes that take place from alien craft while in space. Very rare. Only a handful of successful attempts recorded.	< 0.0001

Although most abductions follow a similar script, the manner of escape from your alien captors is almost infinitely variable. The outcome of your escape bid will ultimately depend on a multitude of factors that are impossible to predict, such as the number of alien hostiles, the location of the abduction attempt, the type and extent of any personal injuries, the nature of the terrain into which you escape, the time of year, whether it is day or night, and what weapons you have at your disposal. Devising detailed contingency plans is, as you can well imagine, extremely difficult. Yet, forewarned is forearmed. Preparation is still your best chance of survival. Therefore, it is important to analyze a range of typical and not-so-typical escape scenarios to familiarize yourself with the diverse range of situations you could encounter.

D.V. Pulbrook, one of the modern fathers of alien escapology research, devised a four-point classification system, known today as the Pulbrook Scale, to describe the disparate range of escapes from alien captivity that have been reported over the last half-century. Each level represents a ten-fold increase in the degree of difficulty and the degree of personal risk.

Levels I and II escapes have the highest success rates, while Levels III and IV represent extreme scenarios where the probability of life-threatening injury, or death, is substantial.

It is important to assess the potential risks involved in any situation you find yourself in before you decide on the appropriate course of action.

LEVEL I: PRE-BOARDING ESCAPES

Boarding passes will not be required during Level I escapes. Sixty-eight percent of all successful escapes have occurred either during initial contact, when the aliens are attempting to paralyze their subjects, or while transporting their captives to their craft. Remember, it is easier to fend off attempted alien mind control than to overcome it once paralyzed. While outside the alien craft, you are still on "home turf," so to speak, and have a distinct tactical advantage.

Also consider that 84 percent of all abductions occur in locations familiar to the abductee. In a familiar environment, you know the lay of the land and can utilize this knowledge in a fight-or-flight situation. Early warning detection devices, such as electromagnetic radiation detectors, can be set and escape routes pre-planned. Field-expedient weapons are more readily available. It is also easier to quickly get out of range of alien electroparalysis fields.

Every endeavor should be made to escape before being taken inside an alien spacecraft.

LEVEL II:
ESCAPING THE CRAFT WHILE STILL ON THE GROUND

Finding yourself onboard an alien spacecraft for the first time can be a frightening and disorienting experience. The very fact that you are onboard would indicate that you have been abducted, and, as a result, are in danger of being subjected to a series of experiments that will negatively impact you and your loved ones for the rest of your lives.

Once taken onboard an alien craft, you will generally have between five and ten minutes in which to escape before lifting off. Airborne escapes are significantly riskier than escapes on the ground, and they rarely end to the satisfaction of the escapee. It is often difficult to tell when you have become airborne in an alien craft as g-force suppression technologies inhibit the human ability to sense motion, no matter how rapid. So it is important to act quickly.

Apart from the inherent dangers associated with the medical procedures carried out by your captors, the spacecraft environment itself presents a few potential hazards. A knowledge of these risks will proove to be invaluable to you during the mayhem of an actual escape.

The primary danger comes from the spacecraft's propulsion systems. While onboard the alien craft, these pose no significant threat, as they are protected within a secure containment area. However, outside the craft, there is risk associated with exposure to the underside of the craft during landing and takeoff. To avoid exposure to high-level electromagnetic fields, it is important that you are at least 50 yards—or preferably 100 yards—from the craft when its engines are operational.

Another potential hazard, although minor, exists in the physical dimensions of the spacecraft itself. Most alien crafts are relatively small in size, with interiors designed for their somewhat diminutive occupants. You may have to double over as you run down the corridor toward the escape hatch and duck under doorways to avoid sustaining a nasty head injury on the architrave. Always watch your step as you exit a spacecraft. Tripping over the spacecraft's landing legs or falling off the end of its gangplank not only is embarrassing, but you could easily twist your ankle, making further escape impossible.

LEVEL III AND LEVEL IV: EXTREME ESCAPES

Escapes do not always go as planned. One moment it may seem that freedom is within your grasp, the next, you are confronted with a situation that appears impossible to survive. If the unthinkable happens, you must be prepared, or, at very least, be familiar with the best course of action and what has worked for others in the past. You must be

THE ALIEN INVASION SURVIVAL HANDBOOK

FACT FILE # *060102HS-08*

FACT FILE NAME: *Foo Fighters*

INCIDENT REPORT:

The term foo fighter was coined by Allied aircraft pilots during World War II to describe a variety of spherical, disc- and wedge-shaped UFOs observed in the skies over Europe and the Pacific. These mysterious ▮▮▮▮▮▮▮ aerial phenomena often followed or flew parallel to aircraft and were known for their remarkable speed and maneuverability, being able to rapidly accelerate or decelerate and abruptly change course.

There is some debate as to the actual origin of the expression foo fighter. Most, however, believe the name is derived from a popular comic strip of the time called Smokey Stover. The main character, Smokey, often said, "Where there's foo, there's fire." A book titled Smokey Stover the Foo Fighter was published in 1938.

Although foo fighters were widespread during the war years, authorities did not consider their ▮▮▮▮▮ behavior to be hostile in nature. One report filed by U.S. Marine Stephen J. Brickner in 1942 states that after an air raid alarm went off in the Solomon Islands, he and his fellow servicemen saw about 150 objects in the sky. They were divided into groups of ten or twelve and were shiny, like polished silver. They wobbled as they moved and were considerably faster than the Japanese aircraft the men were accustomed to seeing. He described the sight

as "the most awe-inspiring and yet frightening spectacle
I have seen in my life."

Foo fighters routinely followed Allied pilots during
▉▉▉▉▉▉ night raids over Germany and France, often
appearing as fiery balls of light. One pilot reported that
a red ball appeared off his wing tip, and was unshakable
until he went into a 350-mile-an-hour dive, at which time
it sped off into the sky.

able to instantly weigh the odds of success, determine your chances of
survival, and make a decision if you are not to risk recapture.

Extreme escapes are a last resort. All other means of evasion
should be attempted first.

How to Survive a Freefall Skydive After Being Jettisoned at 20,000 Feet

First and foremost, think positively. Although survival is improba-
ble, it is not entirely impossible. At least three military airmen have
survived falls from over 15,000 feet without parachutes. Nick Alkemade was a tail gunner in a British Lancaster bomber during World
War II. While returning from a mission over occupied Europe on
March 23, 1944, his plane was hit by enemy gunfire. As the plane

started to spiral out of control and Alkemade was unable to reach his parachute, he decided to leap from the plane rather than burn to death in the wreckage. He fell more than 18,000 feet before hitting

FIGURE 3.1: Utilize freefall maneuvers to reduce your air speed.

the ground. Trees in a pine forest broke his fall before he landed in soft snow. He sustained only minor injuries, including a sprained ankle, and was able to walk away from the scene.

In addition to arming yourself with the assurance that survival is possible, you would do well to remember the following guidelines.

WARNING

Free jumping is a high-risk activity and should not be attempted unless in the most life-threatening circumstances. All other alternatives should be considered before jumping. This is not a procedure that can or should be practiced at home.

---

1. DON'T PANIC. As always, it is imperative that you remain focused and attentive for the three minutes it will take you to reach the ground. Upon exit from the spacecraft, search the terrain below for suitable landing sites.

2. UTILIZE FREEFALL MANEUVERS. It is vitally important that you reduce your air speed as much as possible. This can be achieved by adopting the stable "face to Earth" position. Spread your arms and legs. A falling body reaches a maximum speed, or terminal velocity, of around 120–140 miles per hour. This speed is reached after falling just 1,000 feet. So a fall from 20,000 feet makes no difference to your final impact speed.

3. SELECT A SUITABLE LANDING SITE. This is the key to your survival. The best drop zone will be over a forest, a swamp, snow, or any terrain that can absorb at least some of the impact. Avoid urban areas, exposed hillsides, and agricultural land. Make any in-flight course corrections by shifting your body weight or adjusting the positions of your arms and legs.

4. ADOPT A LANDING POSITION. Keep your body upright and relaxed. Bend your knees slightly and point your toes in the direction of the proposed landing site. Arch your hips in the direction of the proposed roll. Tuck your arms tightly around your head.

5. LAND AS SMOOTHLY AS POSSIBLE. It is important to remember that it's not the 20,000-foot fall that kills you; it's the sudden stop at the end. Contact with the ground should be performed in a single, continuous motion so that the shock is not focused on any one part of the body. Initial contact should be made with the feet, then rolling on one side, the calf, followed by the thigh, buttocks, then diagonally across the back. Remember to keep your head tucked down and your feet and legs together as you roll. Do not use your arms to break your fall; they must protect your head.

6. ASSESS ANY DAMAGE AND RUN FOR COVER. It is highly likely that you will sustain significant injuries upon impact. This, however, should not deter you from seeking immediate cover. Aliens have been known to scour an area for hours looking for escapees. There is no guarantee that concealment will be successful, but at least you don't want to make things easy for them.

How to Survive a Jump From a Low-Flying Spacecraft Into Water

You are onboard an alien spacecraft and have just overpowered your captors. You run down a dimly lit corridor when there is a sudden rush of cold air behind you. Turning around, you see a floor panel sliding open. Looking through it, you see water rushing past, some 150 feet below. Hearing footsteps coming up the corridor, you decide to take your chances and jump through the hatch. You're as good as free ... if you remember these instructions.

1. QUICKLY SCAN THE HORIZON. Avoid the urge to close your eyes. You can accelerate to more than 60 miles per hour in less than four seconds, so you have very little time to prepare for impact. Quickly look around and locate the closest land mass. You will need to swim there after hitting the water.

2. POSITION YOUR BODY FEET DOWN. Hold your legs straight, crossing them at the ankles. Your legs must be firmly clasped together to avoid impact trauma to your genitalia.

3. HOLD YOUR NOSE. To avoid the possibility of a "nasal enema," hold your nose firmly with one hand. Tuck your arm firmly against your body. Use your other hand to hold your first arm tightly in place.

WARNING

Freefall diving is a high-risk activity and should not be attempted unless in the most life-threatening circumstances. All other alternatives should be considered before jumping. The diver must have perfect concentration and timing to enter the water in the correct position. The body is exposed to enormous deceleration forces on impact, and all but the trained athlete will have little chance of survival. If the gods smile upon you and you do survive the impact, then you only have to worry about hypothermia, ocean currents, sharks or crocodiles, exhaustion, and drowning before reaching shore.

4. FACE FORWARD. Tense your neck muscles so that you're looking straight ahead. Make yourself as streamlined as possible by keeping your body straight.

5. ENTER THE WATER FEET FIRST. Entering the water in any other position from this height without extensive training could result in serious injuries or death.

6. SPREAD OUT YOUR ARMS AND LEGS. Once your body has entered the water, spread your arms and legs out to stop yourself from going any deeper. Having plunged into the water at more than 60 miles per hour, you will probably be about 10 feet under the surface. If you find yourself disoriented, follow the bubbles as they ascend to the surface.

7. SWIM TO SHORE. After reaching the surface of the water, turn in the direction of land and begin swimming for shore.

8. SEEK SHELTER. You will need to take evasive action for the next twelve to twenty-four hours. Your alien enemies will undoubtedly be looking for you.

How to Survive in the Vacuum of Space

The likelihood of an unprotected human being surviving in space has been a hot topic for discussion since the 1968 classic science-fiction film *2001: A Space Odyssey*, in which astronaut Dave Bowman "blows" himself from the pod into the airlock without a helmet. How long can a human survive if exposed to the vacuum of space? Would you explode? Would your blood boil? How long would you remain conscious? These are all important questions if you suddenly and unexpectedly find yourself expelled from an alien spacecraft while in orbit.

Although, by its very nature, being alone in the vacuum of space is a frighteningly desperate predicament, there are a number of strategies that will help you regain control of the situation.

1. EXPEL ALL THE AIR FROM YOUR LUNGS PRIOR TO DECOMPRESSION. It is imperative that you do not hold your breath during decompression. Just as scuba divers must remember to exhale as they ascend from the depths of the ocean, you must do the same prior to decompression. The sudden drop of external pressure will cause any air remaining in your lungs to expand rapidly, resulting in the shredding of the soft tissues in the lungs.

2. CHEW SOME GUM. Although usually only a minor annoyance when flying in airplanes or driving in the mountains, blocked ears can pose a serious problem in space. Air pressure in your middle ear is usually the same as your outer ear. The Eustachian tube, a narrow channel connecting the middle ear with the throat, opens periodically in response to swallowing or yawning, allowing air to flow into or out of your middle ear, effectively equalizing the pressure. If the Eustachian tube is blocked due to a common cold, allergy attack, or sinus infection, explosive decompression can result in ruptured or perforated eardrums. Chew gum to help keep your Eustachian tube clear; if that doesn't work, try clearing them by gently exhaling while holding your nostrils closed and keeping your mouth shut.

3. DON'T PANIC. The very thought of perishing within minutes in the cold vacuum of space will cause all but the most stout hearted to tremble. Yet at this time, like no other in your life, you must remain focused on the task at hand and not become distracted by such things as the novelty of zero gravity, the startling clarity of the stars around you, or how you wish you had put on a warm jacket

EXPLOSIVE DECOMPRESSION IN SPACE: FREQUENTLY ASKED QUESTIONS

CAN I SURVIVE?

Yes, if you can fight your way back into the spacecraft within approximately sixty seconds, there is a good chance of survival. Death is guaranteed after two to four minutes.

HOW LONG WILL I REMAIN CONSCIOUS?

From real-life accounts involving decompression in high-altitude aircraft and experimental decompression chambers, it is understood that you will probably have about ten to fifteen seconds of "useful" consciousness. During this time, you will still be able to perform manual tasks with some degree of dexterity. Soon after this, you will lose consciousness due to the lack of oxygen.

WILL I EXPLODE?

The short answer is no. Our skin and blood vessels are strong enough to prevent this from happening. Direct exposure to space for half a minute will not necessarily cause any permanent injury. However, rapid decompression can result in a large pressure differential between the inside and outside of the lungs. If airways are blocked (e.g., if you are holding your breath), the lungs can overexpand, creating pressures capable of rupturing and tearing the delicate tissues of the lungs. This will lead to bleeding, eventually resulting in the lungs being nothing more than a bloody pulp.

WILL MY BLOOD BOIL?

It is true to say that body fluids, including blood, will "boil" in a vacuum, but only in the sense that these fluids turn to vapor. Blood boiling is not an immediate problem for those faced with the vacuum of space. It will not vaporize within the period that you remain conscious because it is protected to some degree by your skin and circulatory system. Body fluids close to the surface of the skin will start to vaporize after ten seconds or so. The saliva in your mouth will begin to "boil" first, then the skin and underlying tissues will start swelling up to twice their normal size. Although unsightly and somewhat uncomfortable, this swelling is not life threatening and will reverse after recompression.

WILL I FREEZE SOLID?

Although the temperature in space is typically very cold (it can fall below −455°F [−271°C]), you will not instantly freeze because heat does not transfer away from the body very quickly. You have enough to worry about in the fifteen seconds of consciousness you have remaining besides turning into a human icicle.

SHOULD I WEAR SUNBLOCK?

Lack of oxygen and tissue injury from decompression and extreme temperatures are not your only concerns while in the vacuum of space. If your bare skin is exposed to direct sunlight, you also risk severe sunburn. Without the protection of the Earth's ozone layer to filter harmful ultra-violet radiation, exposure to sunlight can result in third-degree burns in less than thirty seconds.

HOW LONG WILL I TAKE TO RECOVER?

This depends on a variety of factors, including how long you were exposed. Short-term exposure may include temporary blindness, coughing, and painful swelling. Suffice it to say that you will not be in any physical state to engage in any form of combat with your alien captors until you have fully recuperated.

before leaving home. Your actions within the next few seconds will determine whether you live or die.

4. HOLD ON TO THE SPACECRAFT. Do not let go of the spacecraft. Space is a zero-gravity environment, which means that if you drift out of reach of the spacecraft, there is no way you can get back. You cannot swim through space like in water. Wildly flailing your arms will not move you an inch. The third law of thermodynamics states that for every action there is an equal and opposite reaction. Or, to put it simply, unless you can find something to push against (e.g., a piece of debris from the airlock) to set you in motion back toward the spacecraft, you will continue drifting in space forever. In a pinch, the chewing gum you use to help clear your ears could

THE ALIEN INVASION SURVIVAL HANDBOOK

FACT FILE # *101308XF-15*

FACT FILE NAME: *Project Blue Book*

INCIDENT REPORT:

Government scrutiny of the "flying saucer" phenomenon began in late 1947 with a series of investigations that would last more than twenty years. Project Blue Book was the name given to the longest-running study, which was conducted by the U.S. Air Force between 1952 and 1970. The project was originally led by U.S. Air Force Captain Edward J. Ruppelt. Ruppelt is generally credited with coining the term "unidentified flying object" to replace the previously used "flying saucer" and "flying disc."

The goals of the ▓▓▓▓▓▓▓▓ project were twofold: first, to collect and analyze all available UFO data and, second, to determine if UFOs posed a threat to national security. Of the 12,618 sightings reported during the eighteen years of study, it was concluded that the majority were either conventional aircraft or ▓▓▓▓▓ natural phenomena. While some of the remaining sightings were considered hoaxes, just over seven hundred of the reports—around 6 percent—were classified as unexplained.

Critics of the study claim that it was nothing more than a cover-up, with many of the reports bypassing the project entirely, only to be investigated by other clandestine government authorities. Project Blue Book was the last publicly acknowledged UFO research project conducted by the United States.

also be used to tether you to the spacecraft while you try to open the airlock hatch.

5. USE WHAT TOOLS YOU HAVE AT HAND TO TRY AND RE-ENTER THE SPACECRAFT. Look around you to see if there are any objects that you can use to jam in the airlock hatch as it is closing. The aliens may reopen the door to try and dislodge it, giving you an opportunity to re-enter the spacecraft.

6. TAP ON THE HULL. If the airlock hatch is securely fastened, use any hard object at hand to tap SOS, the international distress signal, on the hull of the spacecraft. Although aliens may not recognize this code, it will alert them to the fact that you are still alive. This demonstration of your tenacity and determination to survive may impress them sufficiently to rescue you as a specimen worthy of further examination. This will provide you with future opportunities to attempt escape in a more conducive environment.

COMMANDEERING AND PILOTING AN ALIEN SPACECRAFT

Forget it. It is pure nonsense to believe that you are capable of flying an alien spacecraft. It may appear easy enough in Hollywood blockbusters such as *Independence Day* or *Star Wars*, but in reality there's a greater chance of you successfully landing a space shuttle blindfolded. Alien aerospace technologies are based on biometric integration with instrumentation specifically designed for their unique anatomy and physiology. They also utilize their powers of electrogenesis to directly control the craft with their minds.

Although some unverified reports indicate that a human may have temporarily gained control of the downed Roswell spacecraft a few moments before impact, no one has ever come forward to substantiate these claims.

EVADING RECAPTURE

Don't think that your problems have come to an end the moment you get out of the alien spaceship and have your feet firmly back on planet Earth. The period of time immediately after your escape is potentially the most dangerous. Aliens are highly motivated to recapture escapees in order to prevent them from sharing with others the knowledge of aliens and their abduction tactics. Even if they decide it's not prudent to study you, aliens will at least recapture you to wipe your memory.

The next twelve to twenty-four hours are critical if you are to avoid detection and subsequent re-abduction. It is during this crucial period that you are most vulnerable, both physically and psychologically. Many succumb to exhaustion during this period and make mistakes. Your response will determine whether you end up as just another abduction statistic or play a pivotal role in humanity's resistance to alien oppression.

ON THE RUN: GENERAL GUIDELINES

1. RUN LIKE HELL. It is important to put as much distance as you can between you and your abductors as quickly as possible. Aliens have not been known to travel on foot more than 600 feet from their spacecraft. Remember, you must be at least 15 feet from them to be outside the range of their electroparalysis.

2. AVOID OPEN AREAS. When on the run from aliens, it is important to avoid isolated roads or trails, open fields, bridges, waterways, and manmade structures, such as sewage plants and public recreational grounds. Aliens tend to assume that you will be drawn to these familiar areas, and will patrol them to recapture you.

3. HOLE UP. Find somewhere to hide as quickly as possible. Utilize any caves or tunnels you find in the local area. If none exist, locate the thickest vegetation you can find. When you have found a suitable hiding place, it is important that you do not go straight to it. Keep some degree of distance, circle around and enter it from a direction other than the one you were originally heading. Try not to disturb the vegetation as you enter. Once you are hidden, sit and listen, scanning the skies for any sign of lights or movement. Remember, most recaptures occur within the first thirty minutes of escape.

4. AWAIT DAYLIGHT. Your escape will probably take place during the night. Nocturnal travel is dangerous. Aliens are creatures of the night in the truest sense. They have highly developed nocturnal vision, which puts them at a distinct sensory advantage. Just because you can't see them doesn't mean they can't see you. Play it safe; wait for daybreak.

5. ASSESS ANY INJURIES. Assess your physical condition. Check your body for any recent cuts or wounds. If any surgically precise wounds are found, suspect the presence of an alien implant. Fresh superficial implants must be removed immediately.

6. HEAD FOR INHABITED AREAS. Your key to survival is to find a large inhabited area as soon as possible. The chances of being re-abducted decrease proportionally to the increase in the number of people around you. Develop a plan of action before you leave your hiding place. Your progress toward an inhabited area will be determined by a number of factors, including your physical condition, and the terrain, vegetation, and climate. Choose an indirect route toward your destination. Make sure that you do not travel in a straight line. Try to make at least one or two dramatic changes in direction along the way. Always choose the most obstacle-free routes with the best cover. Try to travel through areas with the thickest vegetation.

7. USE YOUR INGENUITY. A successful escape will, to a large degree, depend on your ability to think on your feet. Adaptability and decisiveness are your strongest allies when on the run. Utilize any and all available resources at your disposal to achieve your goal.

8. SET TRAPS. When resting, if time allows, setting alien traps (see trap examples in chapter 2) will not only alert you to alien incursions into your "safe zone," but will also, if triggered, act as a deterrent against further pursuit. Position a variety of traps along the most direct routes to your position.

AVOIDING DETECTION
BY ALIEN THERMAL IMAGING TECHNOLOGY

Aliens use a range of technologies to hunt their human quarry, including thermal imaging devices that detect heat energy given off by the body. These instruments make it particularly challenging to evade detection even in the dead of night. They are not fool-proof, however.

First, if you feel that an abduction attempt is imminent while driving a vehicle, stop and get out. Hot engines radiate an enormous amount of heat that is easily traceable. You have a much better chance on foot.

While fleeing a scene, avoid leaving a heat trail. Your body heat is transferred to anything you touch, and these objects can be readily detected as "hot spots" on an otherwise cool background by thermal imaging equipment. Aliens will be able to follow your heat trail like footprints on a beach. Avoid direct contact with your surroundings as much as possible.

You can deceive thermal imaging devices by utilizing available resources to alter your human heat signature. Cover yourself in leaves, mud, or snow as a means of environmental camouflage. Immerse yourself in water. Hide among warm objects that can mask your presence, such as a herd of cows or under an air-conditioning unit. Traveling while it is raining or snowing will also make it more difficult for them to track you.

And finally, remember that thermal imaging devices cannot penetrate through barriers such as domestic walls or dense vegetation. If possible, avoid open areas and hide within enclosed spaces.

Although you may rehearse various escape scenarios to perfection and prepare both your mind and your body for any eventuality, things may not always go according to plan. There may come a time when even your best efforts to escape from the clutches of your adversary are thwarted by circumstances beyond your control. It is at this point that you should stop, turn, and face your enemy. No more Mr. Nice Guy. It's time to get nasty. It's time to go on the attack.

CHAPTER 4

ATTACK

> When you consider attacking, remain calm,
> then suddenly attack first and quickly.
>
> —Miyamoto Musashi

CHAPTER SUMMARY

There comes a time when caution and restraint must be thrown to the wind. You cannot rely on the authorities to come to your aid in a moment of intergalactic crisis. It's up to you, and you alone, to take control of the situation.

You need not be a martial-arts or military-weapons expert to emerge victorious from a physical confrontation with an alien. Once their primary defenses are down, they are no match for the determined human being. Our species has a rich genetic history of violence and, when placed in a dire situation, even the most sedate, mild-mannered individuals are capable of unprecedented and vicious acts of aggression to protect themselves and their loved ones from evil. The rules of civil society do not apply when faced with an alien wielding an anal probe. There comes a time when you must unleash that primal violence that lies dormant in us all. It's simply a matter of changing your mindset: Do you negotiate a truce with a bothersome household fly? Do you try to reconcile the differences of opinion you have with mice in your pantry? Do you seek mediation to resolve the conflict with disease-causing microorganisms? There can be no negotiation, only extermination. Humanity, espe-

cially your own personal slice of it, must prevail at all costs. When interacting with aliens, the word *No!* can be most articulately expressed with a .44 Magnum.

ON THE ATTACK: GENERAL GUIDELINES

Aliens are, by their very nature, unpredictable. You just never know when you will have a close encounter. When an incident occurs, you will not be able to say, "Hang on. I don't have my Smith & Wesson handy. Can you come back in half an hour?" You will be forced to engage the enemy with the resources you have available at a moment's notice. To do this, you must be both physically and mentally prepared.

Our forebears invented throwing sticks, spears, bows and arrows, and intercontinental ballistic missiles for a good reason. The farther you are away from your adversary to deliver a blow, the safer you are. Close proximity to aliens equals danger. Increased distance from aliens equals safety. Whenever possible, utilize weapons and tactics that put as much distance between you and your alien target as possible.

Hand-to-hand combat is a tactic of last resort. Any close combat situation exposes you to the threat of significant personal injury. A misplaced step, a momentary distraction, or indecision, and you could find yourself on the examination slab with your lower alimentary canal open for business.

If it does come to a fight, make sure you throw the first punch. It is vital that you take the initiative in any combat situation. Don't wait for the perfect moment; that may never come. The only way to be safe is to hit first. The element of surprise has been used for millennia to secure an advantage in conflict situations. The upper hand in combat comes in the form of a closed fist.

Aliens are highly intelligent and cunning opponents. They will use every dirty trick in the book in order to win a battle. Many have underestimated their ruthless resolve and suffered the consequences. Their desire to vanquish is as strong as your desire to live. Stay alert and watch your back. Never assume that an alien is no longer a threat just because it is down for the count. Many an unwary human has made this assumption to their great regret. We have all seen the horror movie or thriller where the hero fails to finish off the villain, through some misguided sense of pity or morality. The bad guy invariably recovers just enough to have one last attempt at destroying the hero. Don't let feelings of awe or sympathy cloud your judgment. Take no chances; deliver the final blow for the sake of humanity.

There are no rules governing our interactions with hostile alien forces. Your actions are not bound by any legal conventions, treaties, or ethical restraints. Your response must be what the situation demands. This may or may not include what some people call cruel and unusual treatment. Do the ends justify the means? Only you can determine what is the appropriate course of action in each unique situation. History will ultimately judge whether those actions were warranted in order to save the planet from alien domination. You just have to do what you have to do.

Once you've given it all you've got, get out of there as fast as you can, before the reinforcements arrive. You may prevail against a small number of aliens, but your chances of success are inversely proportional to the number of aliens you engage. Those who fight and run away, live to fight another day. In sum: Hit first, hit hard, then run.

CLOSE-QUARTER COMBAT

Close-quarter combat involves a physical confrontation between two or more opponents, in this case, you and one or more aliens.

This will be the most common form of engagement with the enemy, as most encounters with aliens occur during abduction attempts. Abductions are, by their very nature, up close and personal. These encounters are usually at times when you are off your guard and at your most vulnerable. The alien strategy is to abduct citizens in situations that pose the least amount of threat to themselves. Your greatest asset will be the element of surprise.

Little will they expect that they have selected a human specimen who is not only on to their little game, but prepared to beat them at it. You possess both the knowledge and skills to thwart their insidious plans and turn the tables on their enterprise, sending them packing with their metaphorical tails between their legs.

The goal of close-quarter combat is to be prepared to use either armed (e.g., knife, rifle, baseball bat, potato peeler) or unarmed (hand-to-hand) techniques to vanquish your intergalactic adversaries in as short a time as possible, while incurring minimal injuries to yourself. The nature and amount of force required will depend on many factors.

The goal, however, will always be the same: to defeat your foe. The end result can be either lethal or non-lethal, depending on the desired outcome.

YOUR BODY AS A WEAPON

You will not always be carrying a weapon when confronting your alien foes. Being fully armed in day-to-day situations is not only impractical, but can also be highly undesirable. There is, however, one weapon from which you cannot be parted: your body. With thorough knowledge and training in some basic hand-to-hand combat skills, you will have everything you need to get yourself out of many sticky situations.

ALIEN TARGET ZONES

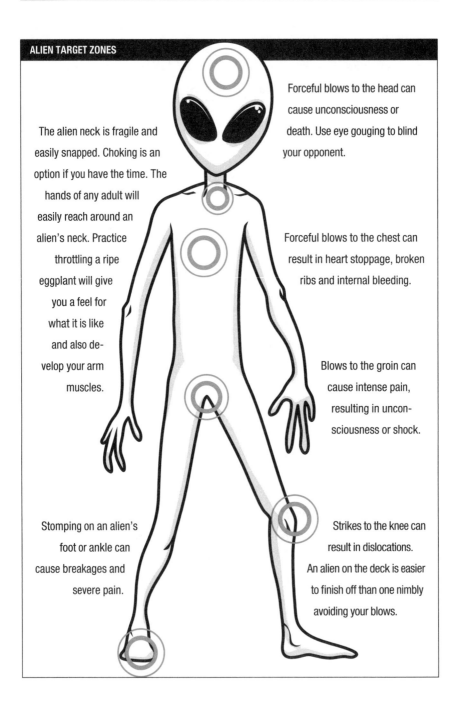

Forceful blows to the head can cause unconsciousness or death. Use eye gouging to blind your opponent.

The alien neck is fragile and easily snapped. Choking is an option if you have the time. The hands of any adult will easily reach around an alien's neck. Practice throttling a ripe eggplant will give you a feel for what it is like and also develop your arm muscles.

Forceful blows to the chest can result in heart stoppage, broken ribs and internal bleeding.

Blows to the groin can cause intense pain, resulting in unconsciousness or shock.

Stomping on an alien's foot or ankle can cause breakages and severe pain.

Strikes to the knee can result in dislocations. An alien on the deck is easier to finish off than one nimbly avoiding your blows.

Fingers: Poking, Ripping, Gouging, Tearing

Fingers are an extremely versatile weapon. They can be used to inflict all manner of nasty injuries on your alien opponent. One obvious target to aim for is an alien's eyes. Eye gouges are achieved by forcefully thrusting the tips of your fingers or thumbs into an alien's eye sockets. This will have the effect of blinding your opponent, providing you with a chance to deliver a fatal blow.

All parts of the eye are equally as sensitive. A particularly enthusiastic gouge may result in your fingers or thumbs penetrating

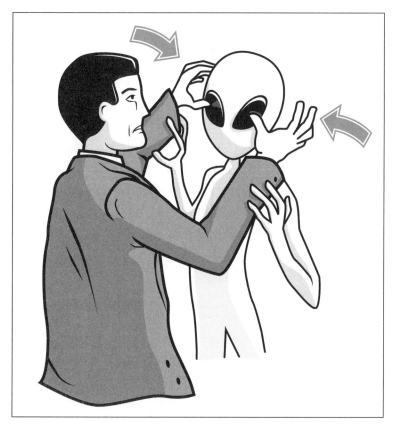

FIGURE 4.1: Use your fingers for gouging.

the eye membrane and sinking into the internal vitreous gel. This feels akin to plunging your thumb into a ripe mango, and, although somewhat unpleasant the first few times, it is not something that should distract you from the task at hand.

Other areas of the alien body are also vulnerable to a digital attack (see sidebar on page 128), but remember, during molting season, an alien skin may peel off in large strips into your hands. Although disconcerting when experienced for the first time, molted alien skin is not dangerous. However, any momentary hesitation on your part may provide aliens with the opportunity they need to gain the upper hand.

Hands: Striking and Punching

Your hands can become formidable weapons during close-range combat. A wide variety of punches and strikes can be used with lethal effect. Although it is possible to strike a lucky blow, your fists, like any weapon, will serve you best if you gain confidence and proficiency through thorough training. Always target your strikes toward your opponents' vital points or nerve motor points. This will have the effect of either taking them out in the first instance or momentarily incapacitating them, giving you an opportunity to finish them off.

Elbow Strikes

Elbow strikes are blows delivered with the point of the elbow or a part of the upper arm or forearm near the elbow. They may be delivered in a downward motion, thrown sideways (either forward or behind), or with an upward thrust. When used properly, the elbows are capable of tremendous striking power and can be used to attack almost any part of an alien's body. The obvious target for an elbow

FIGURE 4.2: Hand strikes can be devastating.

FIGURE 4.3: An elbow can deliver a powerful strike.

strike is the alien's head, but never forget the rib-cracking potential of a blow delivered to the upper torso or the organ-rupturing possibilities of a sharp jab to the abdominal region. Ensure strikes are delivered swiftly and forcefully.

Knee Strikes

The knees are a formidable weapon when wielded with skill and vigor. There is little your flimsy alien adversary will be able to do to defend itself against a barrage of well-placed knee strikes. Knees can be enthusiastically applied while your alien opponent is standing or lying on the ground, cowering for mercy. Try to knee target areas, including your opponent's face, head, ribs, hips, stomach, thighs, or solar plexus. Continue to knee your opponent until it is disabled.

Kicks

Kicking is a very good way of attacking an alien because it allows you to keep some distance between you and your opponent. Plus, your legs contain the largest muscle group and are capable of producing powerful strikes. They are also protected from injury to some degree by footwear.

A combination of kicking and then stomping on a downed alien is sometimes an effective way of bring your disagreement to an end. Remember to use your heel to deliver a volley of targeted strikes to vital areas.

Choking

An adult's hands will easily encircle an alien's neck, which is not much thicker than an average forearm in circumference. If you can wring the water out of a dishtowel, you have all it takes to strangle an alien.

FIGURE 4.4: Knee strikes are a good close-range technique.

FIGURE 4.5: Kicks are devastating and can help maintain distance.

Choking is an effective way of taking the wind out of your adversary's sails. You must, however, be prepared to hold on to a writhing alien's neck for the duration of the ride. As aliens are capable of holding their breath for upward of twenty minutes, you may not have sufficient time to stick around until they lose consciousness.

Rather than targeting the respiratory system, it is usually more efficient to cut off the alien's blood supply to its brain by clenching the arteries on the side of its neck, which can result in unconsciousness within two to three minutes. This period of unconsciousness is somewhat brief. Use this window of opportunity to finish the alien off. A sharp twist to the head by 100 degrees or more will generally suffice, snapping the vertebrae in its neck like a carrot.

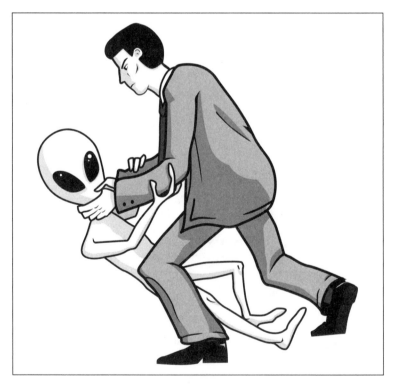

FIGURE 4.6: Use choking to cut off the alien's blood supply.

THE ETHICS OF VIOLENCE: IS IT WRONG TO KILL ALIENS?

When you find yourself in hand-to-hand combat with your alien foes and have the choice of either taking them out or being abducted, violated, and subjected to the gross indignities of forced medical experimentation, the last thing you want to have on your mind is the ethical implications of your actions. You must have no doubt that what you are doing is morally justifiable. When you put that bullet between those two bug eyes, you need to be able to go home and sleep soundly in the knowledge that you've done the right thing.

Humanity has a long and bloody history of butchering other sentient species on Earth for our own benefit. Animals are routinely slaughtered for food, clothes, leather, "vermin" control, and even entertainment and self-aggrandizement. Most of us never give a second thought to the countless beasts that suffer and die so that our species may dominate. No one thinks about the cute lamb frolicking in the fields when we pick up cellophane-wrapped chops at the supermarket. An alien should be afforded as much consideration (meaning, none) while you're dragging a cold blade across its slender neck.

A strange quirk of evolution has resulted in our species holding the power to decide the fate of all other species on planet Earth. Our genetic heritage, crafted by the laws of "tooth and claw" and the survival of the fittest, has given us dominion over all we survey. But our position is tenuous. We must continue to fight for it. We now face an extraterrestrial enemy that, like us, has an indomitable desire to vanquish all "lesser" species, which by their measure includes us. Yet, despite the obvious intelligence and superior technologies of our alien visitors, they are not human, and we are therefore under no obligation to grant them either "human" or "civil" rights. We need not show restraint. We can discharge both barrels with confidence. Murder, by definition, is a word reserved for the deliberate killing of other individuals of our own species. This term cannot be used to describe the intentional killing of aliens.

Questions of ethics, no doubt interesting to philosophers and academics, should not cloud your mind in an alien-conflict situation. The bottom line is, when placed in an "us or them" situation, moral considerations fly out the window. Shoot first, angst later. It is your duty—not only to yourself and your family, but also to your species—to prevail, no matter how great the alien body count.

> Remember, you are not the ruthless tyrant, you are not the relentless oppressor, you're just a guy defending your home, planet Earth. Any planet worth living on is worth fighting for. If the only thing standing between an alien and the rest of humanity is you and a .44 caliber Smith & Wesson, then go ahead ... make my day.

WEAPONRY: ASSEMBLING YOUR ARSENAL

Although few people will have access to military weapons during a close encounter, many will be able to lay their hands on conventional weapons of death: Uncle Albert's hunting rifle, the carving knife you used to cut last Sunday's roast, a screwdriver in the toolbox in the back of your SUV—all can be added to your personal arsenal. Adaptability is the key to success in any tight situation; your resourcefulness will determine who prevails when you unexpectedly come face-to-face with your alien foes.

FIREARMS

The secret to successfully shooting aliens is quite simple: You find them, and you shoot them. This strategy first gained notoriety during the Boer War in South Africa at the beginning of the twentieth century. Harry "Breaker" Morant, an Englishman who enlisted in the Australian Armed Forces to aid the British war against Boer "commandos," was given a directive that any Boers wearing khaki (the color of the British uniform) could be shot on sight. He was subsequently brought to trial over following this order. When asked by the court under what rule he had killed the Boers, he said he had shot them under "Rule 303," a reference to the Lee-Enfield rifle commonly used by the British Army at the time.

Find them and shoot them. Applying this straightforward rule of engagement of our alien enemies is both a simple and effective strategy. If you have the means to take them out, then authority is granted under "Rule 303."

A wide variety of firearms can be successfully employed to ruin an alien's day. The humble BB gun, wielded by skillful hands, can inflict fatal wounds. Even if you're out of ammo, don't turn and run away; you can still use your firearm to bludgeon the offending alien to death.

Don't leave it to the last moment to familiarize yourself with firearms. They are not a weapon for the uninitiated. Join a local gun club and pump off a few rounds every couple of weeks; practice is the key to success. Although you may not need to be able assemble an AK-47 while blindfolded, it would be prudent to be comfortable loading a pump-action shotgun, finding the safety lock on a Smith & Wesson 9mm handgun, and adjusting the sights on a Remington

bolt-action hunting rifle. You never know what firearms may be at hand when you encounter an alien landing craft.

Away from the protection of their spaceship, aliens are sitting ducks. If you have no trouble sinking a few rounds into a watermelon or pumpkin at 50 yards, then you won't have any problem dropping an alien or two. Their heads stand out like neon beacons on a moonless night and are the most obvious targets. Don't bother aiming for their spindly limbs or torso. Not only are these body parts difficult targets due to their size, but gunshot wounds may not result in an instant kill. A clean headshot is usually enough to drop an alien on the spot.

Still, aliens are not always the easiest targets to hit. They can be exceedingly fast and agile, sometimes utilizing a chameleon-like ability to blend into their backgrounds. If they know you're armed, even the most skilled marksman will find hitting one a challenge. Your best chance is a well-planned and well-executed ambush.

BLADES

Bayonets, machetes, knives, scythes, cutthroat razors, and any other implement with a sharp edge are all effective weapons for close-quarter combat, particularly disemboweling or slashing the throat of your alien adversary. However, due caution must be exhibited when using any blade, as sharp-edged weapons are as much a danger to the untrained hand as to the enemy, and in some cases even more so.

The goal of any knife attack on an alien is, of course, to disable it as quickly and efficiently as possible with minimal injury to yourself. To achieve this, attack an alien's vital areas, including the front and sides of the neck, heart, lower abdomen, groin, and face.

Wounds to secondary target areas, such as the legs or arms, can result in substantial blood loss, which, though not immediately fatal, could be sufficient to put your opponent out of commission.

The technique employed during a fight will vary depending on the situation, but it may include a range of basic cutting, slashing, stabbing, and thrusting maneuvers. Remember to apply your full body weight to each stroke, and watch your back for alien reinforcements.

BLUNT WEAPONS

When confronted by an alien with hostile intensions, you must be prepared to utilize whatever you find around you as a weapon, and be willing to do whatever it takes to gain control of the situation. Blunt weapons are available in a multitude of forms in almost any situation you find yourself in. Sticks, baseball bats, golf clubs, billiard cues, chairs, handheld tools, and flowerpots can all be used with lethal effect.

How blunt weapons are used will, again, depend on the circumstances, but combat techniques will generally include striking, thrusting, and choking maneuvers. The impact of a blunt weapon

produces significantly more damage on the delicately framed body of an alien than on a human. For maximum effect, target the alien's head. Blows to its torso and limbs will often result in significant bone breakage, which may deter your alien foe from engaging in further pursuit.

WEAPONS OF OPPORTUNITY

There may be situations when you find yourself in a location with no conventional weapons at hand. At these times, you will have to draw on your ability to improvise and use whatever resources are available. The range of potential weapons at your disposal is only limited by your imagination. Even the humble potato peeler, when wielded by a trained hand, becomes a lethal weapon.

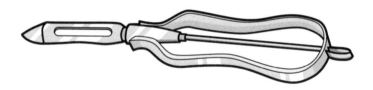

Borrowing From the Toolshed

The average toolshed is a veritable Aladdin's cave of lethal weapons. From the electric hedge trimmer to the two-stroke weed eater, the gardening tools in the corner to the twelve-piece screwdriver set, your potential to unleash carnage on your alien opponent is virtually unlimited. Even ill-equipped sheds usually have all you need to make homemade incendiary devices, such as Molotov cocktails. Your greatest problem: making the right choice.

It is important that you don't grab the first thing in front of you without thinking. You must make your selection with some degree of care and planning. The weapon of opportunity you choose must match the intended use and your level of ability; otherwise, it becomes more of a liability than an asset. Don't grab a chainsaw if you're about to head for the hills on foot and can't carry extra fuel. Lightweight, versatile weapons are best. An ax, for example, can be put to a multitude of uses, not just cleaving alien skulls in two. Be careful not to overlook seemingly insignificant items. Slip a few nails and a coil of wire into your pocket; you never know when you may need them. Also, grab a pair of safety glasses if you have them. They will help to keep body fluids from spraying into your eyes and impeding your vision as you disembowel your alien foe with your trusty hedge trimmers.

Raiding the Pantry

More accidents happen in the kitchen than in any other room of the house. That being the case, the kitchen also presents you with a wealth of potential weapons to ward off an alien attack. Apart from the obvious supply of knives, open a few cupboards and take a look inside; you may be surprised at what you find. Tea towels, oven mitts, or plastic wrap could be used for smothering or choking an alien intruder. A handful of salt or a squirt of dishwashing liquid could temporarily impair an alien's vision, at least long enough for you to bludgeon it to death with your coffee machine. Hurling pots of hot oil or boiling water over an enemy have been a favorite since medieval times and would, no doubt, be as equally effective against aliens. An alien's head could easily be smashed in with a cooking pot or electric waffle maker. Imagine the damage that could be inflicted with skewers, a handheld electric blender, or that toxic green substance at the back of the fridge that you've refused to even look at for the past six months. The possibilities are endless.

IMPROVISED WEAPONS: A BRIEF GUIDE

Take a few moments to walk through your home or office, room by room. Look around you. Try and visualize how the everyday objects you see could be used in a combat situation. This simple preparatory activity will prove to be a valuable timesaver when faced with the mayhem of an alien-encounter situation.

WEAPON: FIGHTING STICK

EXAMPLES: fence pale, umbrella, pool cue, fire poker, tree branch, garden rake

DIRECTIONS: Long, narrow weapons suitable for combat can be found practically everywhere. Improvised fighting sticks are a particularly versatile weapon and can be used for stabbing, prodding, hitting, and poking. They also have the added advantage of putting distance, albeit minimal, between you and your adversary. It doesn't take much of a wallop to snap those fragile alien bones or skewer one of those large gelatinous eyeballs.

WEAPON: KNIFE

EXAMPLES: scissors, broken bottle, garden shears, nail file, razor blade

DIRECTIONS: Anything with a pointed end or sharp edge can be used as an improvised knife. Stab, cut, or slash your alien assailant until it is either incapacitated or dead, then make your escape. Target your attack on soft-tissue areas, such as the throat, groin, or eyes. Take caution with sharp implements, as they can cause you as much injury as they do your enemy.

WEAPON: BLUDGEON

EXAMPLES: vase, electric blender, printer, paving stone, garden gnome

DIRECTIONS: Blunt impact weapons are found in a wide variety of forms in almost any environment. To assess whether an item is suitable or not, ask yourself, "Would that hurt if I were struck over the head with it?" If the answer is yes, then wield it with confidence and vigor.

WEAPON: MISSILE

EXAMPLES: rock, DVD player, kitchen cutlery, hand tool, book

DIRECTIONS: Basically, anything not nailed down can be used as a missile. With small items, it is best to focus on volume rather than accuracy. Throw ten pool balls in a swift volley, and at least one is bound to strike home. Heavy items, such as televisions and bar fridges, can be dropped on unsuspecting aliens from above (e.g., off a second-story balcony or out a window).

WEAPON: GARROTE

EXAMPLES: extension cord, scarf, garden hose, cell phone charger, bath towel

DIRECTIONS: Many rope-like weapons can be found around the average home or office. It need only be relatively thin, flexible, and at least 2 feet in length. Even the common bath towel can serve as a formidable weapon when wielded by trained hands. This multifunctional tool allows you to not only strangle an alien assailant, but also suffocate it if need be. If all else fails, give the towel a few quick twists, and unleash a volley of sharp flicks upon your enemy; we all know how much they can hurt. If nothing else, the alien will be so surprised by this strategy that it will give you a few moments to come up with another plan. Caution should be taken when using small-gauge cords—such as fishing line, electrical wire, or string—as these can result in significant personal injuries.

WEAPON: CHEMICAL

EXAMPLES: cleaning agent, aftershave, petrol, laundry detergent, hot liquid

DIRECTIONS: The modern home is awash with industrial-strength chemicals that have the potential to seriously reduce an alien's enthusiasm for abducting you. Look under your kitchen or bathroom sink, in your laundry cabinet, or on the garage shelf to see what I mean. The skull-and-crossbones symbol is usually a dead giveaway. Aerosol cans can have a similar effect as Mace when used at short range. Remember to aim directly for those two big bug eyes. Once blinded, an alien is easily finished off. A steaming hot cup of coffee or leek and potato soup can ruin an alien's day with little effort. Flammable liquids can be used to make Molotov cocktails or for lighting a protective ring of fire around your home. Remember, having your iPod on full volume will block not only alien electroparalysis, but also the disagreeable screams of an alien burning to death. An alien death cry, described by some as not unlike a squealing pig, is something that can haunt the more sensitive souls for the rest of their lives.

Pilfering From the Office

At first glance, there may not seem to be an armory of weapons at your disposal around the standard office, but look again. The trained eye will spot many mundane and seemingly innocuous items that, when wielded with skill and enthusiasm, can render lethal results. Fax and computer cables can be used to strangle an unsuspecting alien. Desktop telephones make ideal bludgeons. Scissors, letter openers, and receipt spikes all become deadly weapons in the right hands. The adept use of a stapler can render an alien opponent incapacitated within moments. Even a common ballpoint pen can prove a mighty implement of death when attacking vital target zones.

Embracing Vehicular Homicide

Never underestimate the potential of the family car as a weapon of mass destruction. The car reigns supreme as an instrument of carnage in our society, with tens of thousands falling each year before this insatiable killing machine. Three thousand pounds of steel, polymer, and glass can leave quite an indelible impression on the frail body of your alien adversary. But before you put your car into gear and start rolling the steel radials over your first alien speed bump, there are a few things you need to consider. Due caution should always be taken behind the wheel of any motor vehicle. Do not let your enthusiasm for the kill cloud your judgment and threaten your own safety or the safety of other road users. Obey the road rules at all times.

Some may think that running over an alien is the end of the story, but even direct hits are no guarantee of a clean kill. It may be necessary to drive over the body a second or even a third time to finish it off. Driving over an alien's head on a hard surface almost always guarantees a quick kill. These bull's-eyes can generally be distinguished by a loud popping sound beneath the tires.

If a body does not roll out from under the back of your car, stop and carefully check the undercarriage and grill. Body parts can easily get caught up in the undercarriage and will need to be disentangled. Dislodge lumps of alien flesh and gristle from under the car with a stick, and hose off any entrails when you get home. Be thorough; aliens have an uncanny way of tracking missing body parts.

Be wary of alien roadkill. It may be a trap. Aliens have been known to feign death by the roadside and then pounce on hapless do-gooders when they stop to render assistance. Watch for carrion pulling off bits of loose flesh or, if you are still unsure, drive over the body once or twice and see what happens. Fresh alien roadkill can be eaten, if you don't mind a gamey taste. During World War II, two Royal Air Force pilots were forced to live off alien flesh for a week

FIGURE 4.7: Drive over the body a second time.

THE AFTERMATH: LEGAL CONSIDERATIONS AND BEHAVIORAL GUIDELINES

The cold light of reality eventually dawns on us all. If they clap you in handcuffs as you stand amidst a steaming pile of alien corpses, what are your rights? Killing an extraterrestrial is relatively easy. Escaping from the legal aftermath could be your greatest challenge.

However, this may not be as big of a problem as it first appears. There are no national or international laws that govern the treatment of extraterrestrials. So, even if you are caught with a smoking gun, you cannot be charged with killing a creature that, in the eyes of the law, does not exist. Such cases would never get to court. The worst that could possibly happen is a night in a cell, before the federal authorities or special-ops units come in to tidy up the mess made by local law-enforcement officers. The last thing the government wants to do is acknowledge the existence of aliens, for by so doing, they also acknowledge their complicity in the global cover-up. Your case will be quickly and professionally hushed up. Evidence will disappear, witnesses will vanish, official records will be tampered with or removed completely. The official response will be to sweep it under the carpet of public disbelief. Who are people most likely to believe: you, or a host of professionals with letters after their names and spin-doctored scripts?

Even though the chances of prosecution are quite remote, it is prudent to take steps to minimize your implication in any unsavory events. As decision-making can be clouded by heated emotions and general confusion in the aftermath of an alien incident, it is best to have a contingency plan in place. But what's even more important than having a plan is sticking to it when things go crazy.

Your first step must be to put as much distance between yourself and the scene as quickly as possible. Once in a secure location, check yourself for injuries that could be signs of alien implants. Above all else, continue with your daily routine. Although you may have just had the most amazing experience of your life, you must resist the temptation to tell everyone you meet about your alien exploits. Word travels fast when it comes to intergalactic hijinks. Loose lips sink ships. You have enough to worry about with the possibility of alien reprisals without having the Men in Black knocking on your door in the middle of the night. Unless you start making a big song and dance about your experience, the authorities will have little reason to do anything apart from monitor your movements over the next forty-eight hours, in case of any alien payback. So lie low, and maintain a watchful eye for anything out of the ordinary.

when their Lancaster bomber was downed in the French Alps after colliding with a UFO. They described it as being very similar in taste and texture to wild boar and "not altogether unpalatable."

Those with SUVs or other four-wheel-drive automobiles have an opportunity to follow their prey off-road. Bull bars are recommended if you wish to avoid damage to the front end of your vehicle. When driving at night, watch out for the distinctive oval-shaped eyes in your high beams. They are highly reflective and are easily distinguished from other nocturnal animals not only by their shape, but also by their brilliant fluorescent green color.

Do not limit yourself to conventional vehicles; think outside the box. Snowplows, garbage trucks, or combines are all equally effective at flattening an alien. Remember, if you can drive it, you can run over an alien with it.

ALIEN COUNTERATTACK STRATEGIES

Aliens are not totally defenseless. They may not use the heat rays and death machines of science fiction, but they have, when push comes to shove, employed a number of effective defense strategies. This is not to suggest that they are not capable of using advanced weapons against us. Just because they haven't done so to date does not mean they never will. However, it is important to begin with the facts as they are currently known before dealing with any hypothetical situations. For it is by being aware of the full range of an alien's possible responses that we shall be prepared for any eventuality.

SWARMING
Swarming is a term used to describe being engulfed by a seething mass of alien adversaries. Apart from being a very unsettling

THE ALIEN INVASION SURVIVAL HANDBOOK

FACT FILE # *040808PM-17*

FACT FILE NAME: *The Men in Black*

INCIDENT REPORT:

Long before the success of the 1997 film, the term Men in Black was used by UFO conspiracy theorists to describe the ▓▓▓▓▓▓▓▓ mysterious individuals who appeared shortly after UFO sightings to intimidate witnesses into remaining silent.

Described as being Oriental in appearance, hairless, and wearing Blues Brother-esque black suits and ties with starched white shirts, the Men in Black travel in mint-condition black Cadillacs. Their identity, though still unknown, has been linked to various ▓▓▓▓▓▓▓ government agencies and even extraterrestrial entities.

The expression itself was first used by the pioneering UFO investigator Albert Bender, who, in 1953, was instructed by "three men wearing dark suits" to cease publication of his small-circulation flying saucer magazine. He felt so menaced by their ultimatum that he couldn't eat anything for two days and finally closed the magazine. The Men in Black have since appeared to many ▓▓▓▓▓▓▓▓ around the world, using verbal coercion and warnings of dire consequences if their message is not heeded.

experience, it has proved fatal in a number of encounters. In this alien form of "stacks on the mill," you are overpowered by the sheer mass of bodies. Fending off two or three aliens is eminently feasible, but holding back a tide of thirty or forty is well nigh impossible. If you don't die of asphyxiation, you can literally be pulled limb from limb. Luckily, this form of counterattack is relatively rare, as most alien scouting parties consist of only three or four individuals, but it does happen. If unarmed, the best course of action is to run like hell.

HERDING

Like Plains Indians herding buffalo into a ravine, aliens can utilize local geographic features to their strategic advantage. In this variation of swarming, you can be swept along by a living alien tsunami toward a precipice, cliff face, or wall—or any sharpened projections, such as tree branches or rusted agricultural machinery—then cast un-ceremoniously to your doom.

This form of attack presents some serious problems for the unarmed combatant. Struggling against the forces of physics is futile. Dropping to the ground will only result in either you being stampeded to death or the aliens changing their tactic to a swarming maneuver.

Despite its reputation as an end-game tactic, the "conveyor belt of death," as it has been called by some, is known to have been defeated on at least one occasion. In this instance, a Dutch tourist on the island of Viti Levu, Fiji, escaped a stampeding mob of aliens by clawing his way to the top of the alien throng and scrambling across their heads, like a rock star in a mosh pit, and then making a frantic dash through a banana plantation to safety.

HIT AND RUN

As the title implies, this counterattack measure involves aliens swiftly running from cover, striking you, and dashing off again before you know what's hit you. The aim seems to be an attempt to disorient you and increase the chances of you falling and injuring yourself, providing them with an opportunity to pounce. This strategy is usually used when there are two to five aliens in an attack. One will keep you distracted while the others swoop in for the strike. Stay low, watch your back, and head for cover as quickly as you can.

EYE GOUGE

When it comes to individual hand-to-hand combat, aliens are at a distinct disadvantage. Physically weaker than us, they must rely on damaging our most vulnerable soft-tissue areas to inflict any substantial injury. Our eyes are a prime target for attack. Gouging or tearing the eyes with fingers or other instruments can result in permanent eye injury and visual impairment. If you anticipate a clash with extraterrestrials, protective eyewear is highly recommended.

TESTICLE SQUEEZE

Another obvious target for alien attack is the genitalia. Aliens have a wealth of experience with human genitals and are fully aware of their vulnerability. An alien attack on your groin is not a pretty sight. It is considered by most as the coup de grâce of counterattacks and may involve hitting, punching, squeezing, kicking, grappling, stomping, biting, or using handheld weapons. These attacks can cause immense pain and instant debilitation, effectively putting you at their mercy. Your groin must be protected at all costs; the future of humanity may depend on it.

NIPPLE TWIST

Females are not immune to gender-specific alien assaults. There have been a number of recorded incidents, most recently during the late 1990s, of aliens making strategic strikes on females' nipples. These mammary lunges all occurred in situations in which aliens have had their metaphorical backs to the wall. Although their intentions were at first misconstrued by some, a pattern soon emerged that warrants taking adequate precautions. Firm sports bras are recommended in combat situations, particularly in cold weather.

HANDHELD WEAPONS

Although uncommon, aliens have been known to utilize field-expedient weapons during combat, such as sticks, rocks, and unsecured gardening equipment. They do, however, seem to have an aversion to wielding handheld weapons and will do so only as a last resort. Their handling skills are generally clumsy, and any injuries they do inflict are often the result of luck rather than good technique. Mishandled weapons have, on occasion, resulted in some rather nasty self-inflicted injuries. Aliens wielding weapons of convenience are generally more of a threat to themselves than they are to you. Most demonstrations of alien bravado with weapons are nothing more than sheer bluff. When confronted with an alien brandishing a lamp stand or golf club, take whatever measures you deem necessary to disarm them, literally.

WE WILL PREVAIL

Deprived of their powers of paralysis, aliens have a lot to worry about. With their historical advantage eliminated, humanity has the opportunity to show them what we are truly made of. We haven't clawed our way to the top of the evolutionary tree only to be usurped by some officious, gray-assed beings from outer space. Being the dominant species on the planet is not a position that should be taken lightly. If we are to maintain our status, we must take the gloves off from time to time and get our hands dirty. The secret to launching a successful attack against our alien foes is to dispense with any preconceived notions of civility or fair play. Hit first and hit hard. There are no holds barred in interstellar conflict. So, bring it on, baby. Let's rock.

THE ALIEN INVASION SURVIVAL HANDBOOK

FACT FILE # *197307XH-11*

FACT FILE NAME: *Area 51*

INCIDENT REPORT:

Area 51, also known as Dreamland, is a secret U.S. ▇▇▇▇▇▇▇▇▇▇ research facility located near Groom Lake in a remote corner of the Nevada desert (about 90 miles north of Las Vegas). Originally chosen as a testing ground for Lockheed's U-2 spy plane during the 1950s, it has grown to take center stage in modern UFO and government conspiracy theories. The region around the facility is a designated "restricted area" and is permanently off-limits to the public. The perimeter of this facility is protected by an elaborate array of hi-tech surveillance equipment and armed guards with a shoot-to-kill mandate. The base is reputed to have not only one of the world's largest ▇▇▇▇▇▇▇▇ aircraft hangers, but also one of the longest runways in the United States. The area is also alleged to house an extensive underground research facility.

There has been much speculation about the classified ▇▇▇▇▇▇ research being carried out at the base, with claims including the storage of crashed alien spacecraft, reverse engineering of alien technologies, and the study of alien specimens, both living and dead.

Some believe that the secret projects once carried out there have been moved to other facilities, and that Area 51 is now no more than a decoy.

16777XR-19
The Washington National
Airport Incident

CHAPTER 5

INVASION

> We are waiting for the long-promised invasion.
> So are the fishes.
>
> —Winston Churchill

CHAPTER SUMMARY

When all hell breaks loose during an alien invasion, you will invariably find yourself in situations unenvisaged by even the most talented Hollywood screenwriters. We can only imagine the fiendish devises and cunning strategies that the aliens will employ to subdue the nations of the world. Yet, do not despair. The future of humanity will rest on your ability to keep a clear head and a single-minded resolve to prevail, no matter what the odds.

In 1955, Gen. Douglas MacArthur is reputed to have said, "The nations of the world will have to unite, for the next war will be an interplanetary war. The nations of the earth must someday make a common front against attack by people from other planets." While the threat of an alien invasion may not weigh too heavily on our minds as we go about our day-to-day business, there are many who believe that preparations for this conflict are now in their final stages and that an alien invasion is only a matter of time. Although no one knows when or how this invasion may occur, it is important that we are not caught unprepared.

Preempting an attack from an adversary whose military capabilities we know nothing about may, at first, seem an overwhelming challenge, but we are not totally in the dark. We can draw inspiration from the wealth of experience provided by some of the world's most fertile imaginations who can conceive of and understand, far better than we, what we may be facing. For what is today's science fiction is often tomorrow's reality. However, this chapter must be premised with a warning: Unlike what has preceded in this book, what follows is mere conjecture. The advice given here is not based on real-life experiences or hard scientific and historical facts. So, it is important to remember that when the aliens do come, it may be in ways that we have not anticipated. You must be willing to adapt to new situations. Humanity will prevail on its wits, courage, and indomitable will to survive. We must never forget that, as Thomas Paine said, "The harder the conflict, the more glorious the triumph."

WHY WOULD ALIENS INVADE?

Before considering how to best prepare for and survive an alien invasion, it would be prudent to consider why they would want to invade in the first place. The motivating forces behind any invasion will, to a large extent, determine the manner of execution of that invasion, with the resulting implications for humanity. Although many paths lead to Rome, each approaches from a different angle. A well-planned defensive strategy will take into account every possible variation of attack, as each presents its own unique set of challenges. The following is list of ten possible reasons why aliens may someday invade Earth. It is by no means definitive, but it can act as a general guide from which we may base further speculation.

1. RESOURCES: Although rarely acknowledged, resource acquisition is one of the most common reasons for invading countries and, for that matter, planets that do not belong to you. If through ineptitude, greed, misadventure, or natural calamity the resources of your own country or planet have been depleted to uncomfortable levels, then all you have to do is take someone else's. This is nothing but simple playground bully logic. Our own species has a long and bloody history of subjugating the hapless inhabitants of less powerful nations for the acquisition of their resources. Whether they raid Earth for our minerals, water, or biota, be assured humans will be considered a hindrance to the primary goal and therefore, will be ultimately expendable.

2. RESETTLEMENT: There are many reasons why aliens may be forced to leave their home planets, including persecution, war, natural disasters, overpopulation, terrorism, or depletion of natural resources. Just as our pilgrim fathers set forth toward a new world of opportunities, intergalactic refugees will also be on the lookout for hospitable new homes. As Earth is the most livable planet in this neck of the galactic woods, it would be an obvious target for resettlement. With an enviable climate, by interplanetary standards, and more

THE ALIEN INVASION SURVIVAL HANDBOOK

FACT FILE # *1673zXR-19*

FACT FILE NAME: *Bee Abduction*

INCIDENT REPORT:

Colony Collapse Disorder (CCD) is a relatively recent phenomenon in which large numbers of worker bees from commercial beehives abruptly and mysteriously disappear. CCD was first noted in bee colonies in North America in late 2006, followed by similar reports across Europe and Asia. As honey bees are responsible for the pollination of a wide variety of commercial crops, the CCD phenomenon could result in the loss of billions of dollars from the U.S. agricultural market alone. The disappearances have been attributed to a wide variety of causes, including radiation from cell phones, environmental-change-related stresses, pesticides, genetically modified crops, mites, malnutrition, and a variety of exotic pathogens.

By mid-2007, another more compelling explanation arose out of California's almond-growing heartland, the Great Central Valley. Walt Strömbergsson, a sixty-five-year-old apiarist and regional Boules champion, was on his way to relocate some hives on a local orchard just outside the town of Hilmar, Merced County, when he observed a large metallic disc hovering above the treetops. He stopped his car and watched as a small panel opened beneath the ▬▬▬▬▬▬▬ craft and a narrow tube descended to within inches of the hives. He later said, "Damndest thing I ever seen. It was like a giant alien vacuum cleaner. Just sucked those bees right up, then took off." Upon inspecting the hive, he discovered the whole colony had been taken.

Similar incidents have been reported from various localities across North America and from as far afield as France and Taiwan. Although authorities are quick to dismiss them as pranks or atmospheric anomalies, there are those who believe that we are witnessing a new wave of ▨▨▨▨▨▨ alien abductions.

While the widespread, systematic abduction of humans began in the 1960s and of frogs during the 1990s, bees appear to be the next life-form on the aliens' hit list. Why aliens have taken an interest in our honey-producing friends is anyone's guess, and only time will tell whether they are returned unscathed from their ordeal.

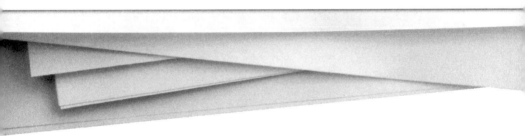

resources than you can poke a stick at, our planet has a lot going for it. The only thing possibly interfering with a successful alien relocation program is a pesky infestation of *Homo sapiens*. That won't be a major problem. We all know how indigenous populations are usually dealt with in these situations.

3. FOOD SOURCE: Shining like the proverbial golden arches in the unfriendly wastelands of deep space, Earth unwittingly sends an open invitation to all those in the galactic neighborhood to come and dine at our expense. Our planet offers the ravenous alien traveler a veritable smorgasbord of organic delights. With an unparalleled selection from a seething multitude of life-forms, Earth could become the most popular fast-food outlet in the solar system. So, whether it be to harvest the plant and animal life or to imbibe the juices of our own species, when they come, you better hide the knives and forks.

4. FORCED LABOR: It is not outside the bounds of reason to suggest that aliens may wish to avail themselves of our rich potential as an unpaid labor source. We, as a species, possess many attributes that make us ideal workhorses for interstellar taskmasters. We are intelligent, quick to learn, readily adaptable to new environments, capable of great feats of brute strength (just look at the pyramids), and, above all, numerous and there for the taking. Just as we continue to exploit the services of so-called "lesser" species on the planet, aliens may find a multitude of disagreeable, mundane, or hazardous tasks within their own society to which, with a little bit of encouragement, we would be eminently suited. Indeed, slavery and various forms of bonded labor have been used by so-called "civilized" societies for millennia to advance the interests of dominant cultures. It is not a great leap to suggest that those who enslave may also one day be enslaved.

5. REFUGE: Rogue military outfits and garden-variety criminals have an unfortunate habit of heading for the hills when their fiendish plots don't work out as planned. Aliens on the run from intergalactic law-enforcement agencies will be looking for a convenient hideout in a remote and inconspicuous part of the galactic neighborhood. Just as Fletcher Christian and his fellow mutineers aboard the British HMS *Bounty* chose isolated Pitcairn Island in the South

Seas to hide from the wrath of the imperial powers, aliens who have fallen foul of the law may think all their Christmases have come at once when they set their eyes on our uncharted planet. Although Earth is inhabited by a few billion bipedal primates who are at a stage of development where they still think cell phones are a pretty neat idea, they're not likely to pose too much of a problem for a ruthless band of ray-gun-wielding cutthroats.

6. PROSELYTISM: It would not be unreasonable to assume that religion, in more bizarre forms than we could possibly imagine, pervades the conscious cosmos. Fundamental to most forms of religion is the vehement belief that their particular understanding of the great unknown is right and everyone else's is wrong. This often forms the basis of a campaign to convert others to their own view of things. If this isn't successful, the unbeliever is shunned or ostracized. Some more primitive religions bypass these stages altogether and go straight for the extermination of the unbeliever.

Throughout history, proselytism has also been used as a pretext for invading and plundering foreign countries. If the heathen don't accept our view of the universe, then they don't deserve the rich natural bounty our gods have provided for them. It's a simple matter of redistribution of wealth to those whose god has blessed them with the biggest guns or heat rays, as the case might be.

There are no antagonists more fearsome or committed to their objectives than those who believe their actions are sanctioned by their gods. If you want a picture of the future, imagine a fist, wrapped in holy scripture, smashing a human face—forever. Let us hope alien invaders are atheists.

7. PENAL SETTLEMENT: There's no better way of disposing of those undesirable elements in our society than to send them off to another

THE ALIEN INVASION SURVIVAL HANDBOOK

FACT FILE # *16743XR-01*

FACT FILE NAME: *Ancient Arrivals*

INCIDENT REPORT:

The Wandjina are the haunting "sky beings" or "cloud spirits" of Australian aboriginal mythology. With their large, dark eyes and ▓▓▓▓▓▓▓▓ spindly limbs, they bear a striking resemblance to the ▓▓▓▓▓▓▓▓ alien form we are most familiar with today. Depicted in numerous ancient rock-art and cave-painting sites around ▓▓▓▓▓▓▓▓ Australia, they are the "spiritual ancestors" that are "born of the dark." They continue to visit the native inhabitants in some of the most remote areas of the outback even today.

country or, for that matter, another planet. Out of sight, out of mind, as the saying goes. It worked well for the British Empire in the eighteenth century, so why wouldn't it work with a motley crew of alien miscreants as well? All you need to find is a suitable planet in the unfashionable backwaters of the galaxy and clear out the locals to make way for the first shipment. It couldn't be simpler.

8. SPORT: On Earth, *Homo sapiens* have the dubious honor of being the only species that kills other sentient beings for entertainment. Spanish bullfights, duck shooting, and big-game hunting all testify to a perverse primal blood lust that we have yet to shake from our genetic heritage. Hunters will go to no end of trouble and expense to pop a few rounds into some hapless deer or antelope, lop off its head, stick it up on the living room wall, then stand there gloating over the pitiful carcasses, espousing their virility and triumph over the lesser creatures. We may not be alone in this desire for wanton, mindless carnage, though. At this very moment, on a planet in a not-too-distant star system, some redneck alien may be stowing the trusty laser blasters in the trunk of its flying saucer and checking its star map for the quickest route to Earth.

Our planet may someday be one giant *Homo sapiens* theme park where intrepid intergalactic hunters don their silver spandex safari suits and prepare for a chest-thumping body count. We can only imagine the assortment of human body parts that may someday adorn an alien's living room walls as macabre trophies of his dominance over lesser life-forms.

9. DIVING INTO THE GENE POOL: Scientists have long been aware of the important role that a wide ancestral gene pool plays in the hereditary health of a population. Having a large variety of mates to choose from provides the genetic diversity required by natural selection to reduce the number of mutations that weaken the long-term viability of a population. The concept of human-alien hybrid experimentation is not new to ufologists and may represent a last-ditch effort to introduce new vitality into an ailing alien population. When their experiments and breeding programs are complete, they may initiate an invasion to provide a home for their newly created legions of genetically modified half-breeds.

10. SEXUAL ADVENTURE: Although it may seem a long way to come for cross-species liaisons, much talk has, over the years, been made of the sexual exploits of our intergalactic visitors. As we all know, primal sexual urges make creatures do crazy things. It is, by no means, impossible to imagine hormone-driven aliens cruising the planet on a Saturday night in their freshly waxed and polished flying saucers looking to sample some of the Earthly delights of our primate society. When it comes to the realm of sexual conquest, there are few boundaries. Aliens may gladly put our genetic difference aside in the pursuit of pleasures of the flesh.

POINTS TO CONSIDER
IN PREPARATION FOR AN ALIEN INVASION

We can expect a full-scale alien invasion to be unexpected, swift, and merciless. Aliens know their stuff. They have been conducting surveillance operations on Earth for a long time. They are fully aware of our military capabilities and strategies. They will have the upper hand. They know our weak spots and will exploit them without hesitation. We will most likely be caught totally off guard in such a way that all may seem hopeless. Although civilization as we know it today may collapse, it is from this chaos that the seed of human ingenuity will sprout and we shall arise from the ashes as victors.

Take these steps prior to an invasion so that you can worry less during an alien attack.

SECURE ELECTRONIC DEVICES

One of the most serious threats to a nation's ability to protect itself from alien invaders comes from the possible use of electromagnetic pulse weapons against our technological infrastructure. The devastating power of electromagnetic pulses was first observed during high-altitude nuclear weapons detonations during the Cold War era, and it has been a concern to military researchers for well over thirty years. Apart from the ability to instantly kill thousands of people, it was discovered that nuclear detonations also have the capacity to disrupt or destroy electronics systems. A single, high-intensity, broadband, short-duration burst of electromagnetic energy at an altitude of 300 miles could effectively bring the continental United States to its knees within moments, without any direct fatalities. These electromagnetic pulses, or EMPs, create power surges that have the ability to damage or destroy all unprotected electrical equipment, global communications networks, and even entire power grids.

Although the military has preparations well under way for an EMP attack, civilian targets are largely unprotected and susceptible to widespread failure. Recovery from such an attack would take years, if not decades, even under the most ideal conditions. Although engineering protection into new products and structures may only add a few percent to the overall cost, hardening and retrofitting unprotected systems could be both difficult and expensive. The most effective method is to encase sensitive equipment in an

THE ALIEN INVASION SURVIVAL HANDBOOK

FACT FILE # *13763XB-13*

FACT FILE NAME: *The Washington National Airport Incident*

INCIDENT REPORT:

The summer of 1952 provided Washington, D.C. with a series of unidentified flying object incidents that are among the most documented and credible of all time.

On the evening of July 19, 1952, air traffic controllers at Washington National Airport spotted several unidentified ▮▮▮▮▮▮▮ objects on their radar screens. Visual confirmation was soon made with a number of bright orange lights visible in the night sky. These objects fanned out across the capital, circling over several prohibited flying zones, including the airspace over the White House. Andrews Air Force Command was immediately contacted, and they confirmed the situation was being monitored and response aircraft had been scrambled.

The objects moved erratically, executing abrupt 90-degree or 180-degree turns within moments and reaching speeds of up to 7,000 miles per hour. At one point, one of the objects shadowed a commercial airliner that had just taken off.

For the next five hours, the objects played a cat-and-mouse game with the U.S. Air Force jets sent to intercept them. Although the pilots made distant visual contact with their targets, the ▮▮▮▮▮▮▮ objects disappeared the moment they tried to approach. Numerous witnesses detailed seeing fiery orange spheres and huge discs

flying in formation above their heads. The sighting made
front-page headlines in newspapers across the country.

A week later, on the evening of July 26, the crew of a
National Airlines flight into Washington, D.C. witnessed
███████████████████████████ strange lights above
their aircraft. The objects were confirmed by radar at
Washington National Airport and Andrews Air Force Base,
whose crews were also tracking several other unidentified objects in the vicinity. Jets were again scrambled to
intercept the UFOs. Although the objects were elusive, at
one point they surrounded one of the fighter jets before
breaking off and disappearing at high speeds.

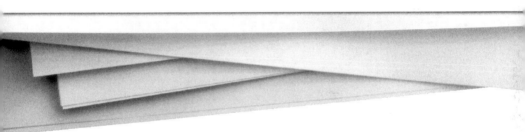

electrically conductive enclosure, such as a Faraday cage, which
prevents the pulse from accessing it. However, this method is not
foolproof, as any lines that run into the equipment—such as power cords, antennas, and modem cables—can act as an entry point
for an EMP power surge. These external connections must also be
coated in wire mesh or some other conductive material. Although
commercially available surge protectors may offer some degree of
protection under low-intensity strikes, they must be used as part of
a complete protective system to be effective.

BURY YOUR VALUABLES

When the aliens come, you will likely be forced to abandon your home. Any treasured family heirlooms or valuables are best buried as a precaution against looters. Choose a container that is made of non-biodegradable plastic and has a lid that is completely watertight. Remember to take careful note of its position in relation to local landmarks, as it may be some time before you can return to retrieve it, and at that point your neighborhood may no longer be recognizable.

FAMILIARIZE YOURSELF WITH LOCAL INFRASTRUCTURE

If you are stuck in a city during an alien attack, you may be forced to hide out in sewers or subway tunnels (see "Go to Ground" on page 171). Get on the Internet now or visit your local government offices to obtain the relevant local subterranean maps. Memorize them; you may not have a map on you when the attack begins. Check the location and condition of manhole covers and other entry points in your neighborhood; practice finding them in the dark. Are they easy to remove? Do you need a crowbar or other specialized tools? Make sure you know alternative exit points as well as "safe zones" within the system that can be used to escape high storm-water levels. Be prepared for human competition for these sanctuaries; your neighbors may prove to be more of a threat to your safety than the aliens in these coveted locations.

TIPS FOR SURVIVING AN INVASION

We know it only takes a single blast from a heat ray to blow your home to kingdom come, so there is little point in boarding up the windows. Although some of the simple precautions here and in chapter 2 may prove effective against alien abductions, alien military attacks are a whole different ball game. Domestic, commercial, and industrial buildings will be a focus for their attacks. Basements may offer some degree of protection at the outset of an invasion, but your best defense is to leave your home, or any other dwelling, as soon as possible after the initial attack. Make sure you have all your provisions ready to go. A well-prepared survival kit will be essential and should include:

- supplies and tools to keep you warm against the elements (e.g., space blanket, raincoat, waterproof matches)
- enough freeze-dried food to last at least a week, a canteen, and a water filter
- a first-aid kit
- navigation equipment, including maps and a compass (remember, global positioning systems probably won't work)
- an MP3 player and ample spare batteries for each member of your party
- lightweight weapons (e.g., handgun, knife, machete), for when things get rough

Pets may become valuable allies during an alien invasion. Their keen senses may alert you to the presence of extraterrestrials long before visual contact can be made. This must be weighed, of course, against the possibility that the family dog's barking may expose your position, thus making it easier for the aliens to track you.

HEAD FOR THE HILLS

The safest place to be during an alien invasion is away from major urban centers. The world's cities and towns will be the focus of an initial alien attack, followed by mop-up operations in smaller regional centers. The farther you are away from other people, the better. Head for isolated rural locations or wilderness areas. Backcountry cabins and remote rural homesteads will provide sanctuary for a while, but also be prepared to evacuate these at a moment's notice. Expect competition from other refugees for accommodation. Your biggest threat, apart from the aliens, will be from desperate gun-toting brigands who will want to take advantage of your preparations. Avoid the fleeing masses as much as possible.

FIGURE 5.1: Major cities will likely be the focus of initial alien attacks during an invasion.

SEEK ALTERNATIVE FORMS OF TRANSPORTATION

As electromagnetic pulses (EMPs) can permanently immobilize vehicles with electronic ignitions and control systems, we must assume that you won't be able to make a quick getaway in your SUV after an alien invasion. Don't bother changing the solenoid in your vehicle, as EMPs usually only damage electronic circuitry, and it would most likely be unaffected.

You and millions of other people will all be attempting to get out of the major urban centers at the same time, probably on foot. Your escape will need careful planning and preparation. Consider the use of older vehicles without electronic circuitry. Also consider the use of man- or animal-powered vehicles. Now is the time to oil that rusty bicycle chain.

CHOOSE UNCONVENTIONAL ROUTES

Whenever you're fleeing from alien pursuers, the most straightforward route is never the safest. Similarly, following a crowd of your neighbors is just asking for trouble. During an alien invasion, there will be no safety in numbers. In fact, quite the opposite will be true. Use the road less traveled. Minor country roads, forestry tracks, and even waterways offer greater chances of escaping unscathed. Remember, your goal is to isolate yourself from the mass of humanity as quickly as possible.

GO TO GROUND

Subterranean environments, such as caves and mining shafts, make ideal fortresses against invading aliens. They provide protection not only from being located, but also from "death rays" and other forms of alien weaponry. They can also act as a base from which to

launch your guerrilla campaign against the alien invaders. Forays can be made above ground for food and other essentials.

Those who have, for whatever reason, remained behind in the city can utilize underground drainage and sewage systems for shelter. Don't wait, however, until the invasion begins to try and locate these underground facilities (see "Familiarize Yourself With Local Infrastructure" on page 168).

HOW TO OUTWIT ALIEN DEFENSE SHIELDS

Apart from the Rosenberg incident in 1953, there have been few documented cases of humans coming in direct contact with "force fields" during alien encounters. Most of us would be familiar with the concept of alien defense shields from such notable science-fiction films as *War of the Worlds*, *Independence Day*, and the various reincarnations of *Star Trek*. Sometimes depicted as being electromagnetic in nature, these defensive shields typically form a protective and often invisible barrier around alien spacecraft that is impervious to all forms of conventional weaponry.

As this technology has not, as yet, been developed on Earth (to our knowledge), it is impossible to provide a detailed analysis of how force fields work or comprehensive strategies for combating them. This should not preclude us from devising contingency plans for the situations in which we may encounter them, however. It's always better to be safe than sorry.

Here are some points to remember:

- Attempts at penetration are futile. Force fields are, by their very nature, designed to be formidable obstacles in combat situations. There is little point in the average person trying to discover ways to penetrate them. That is a job best left for the military. We do not have the time or the resources to cross technological swords with our alien foes. We must rely solely on our wits.

- Attempt infiltration. Rather than trying to batter your way through a brick wall, simply walk around it. The easiest solutions are usually the best. While going through a force field may be well nigh impossible, sneaking around the edges of one is feasible. Use your imagination. Allow yourself to be captured and taken onboard, disguise yourself as an alien, and bypass alien security checkpoints. It may just work; it does in Hollywood. Your most important resource is your adaptability and your will to succeed.

- Strive for total sabotage. Getting onboard is only half the battle. You still need to disable the force field. This is a

task in which you cannot afford to be too subtle. It is reasonable to assume that you do not know where the "off" button is, and will, therefore, need to take more drastic steps. The generators responsible for producing the force fields are never near the hull, so you will have to go deep inside the ship. You would probably not recognize a force field generator if you saw one, so the most prudent course of action is to destroy as much of the hardware you encounter as possible. How you do this will depend on the resources you have at your disposal and on your own ingenuity.

- Get out alive. You needn't worry about going down with the ship if you destroy the wrong machinery; those who are willing to sacrifice all for the good of humanity usually make it out alive at the last moment. It would, however, be worth your while to take careful note of your route while penetrating the maze of corridors in the inner sanctum. Your departure will be made in great haste with a horde of pissed off aliens in hot pursuit. The last thing you want under these circumstances is the inconvenience of having to stop and decide if you should take the passage to the left or the one to the right.

HOW TO SURVIVE ALIEN DEATH RAYS

Death rays are a type of directed energy weapon that have long been portrayed in science fiction. They have been known under a variety of names, including heat rays, ray guns, phasers, blasters, and laser guns. First described in H.G. Wells's 1898 book, *The War of the Worlds*, they have in recent years become the focus of military research and development. Although current prototypes are not to the stage of instantly vaporizing their targets, tactical lasers are showing great potential as a defense against enemy missile and artillery attacks.

Alien death rays, however, are another story. This highly developed alien technology is a formidable weapon and should not be underestimated. Here are a few strategies that can be employed to reduce the chances of getting fried.

- Avoid the line of sight. Death rays travel in a straight line, which means that if you are not in an alien's direct line of sight, you cannot be hit. However, that is not to say that there is no danger of being struck from flying debris or shrapnel from nearby objects that are hit.

- Monitor your surroundings. Not being able to see an alien gunship doesn't necessarily mean that you are safe. Ray guns can be fired from incredible distances with pinpoint accuracy. Death rays travel at the speed of light, and once they are fired, you can be fried before you know what's going on. A general rule of thumb is to watch what's going on around you. If others are turning to dust before your eyes and buildings are exploding in flames around you, it's probably a good idea to run for cover.

- Seek appropriate shelter. Your best chance of surviving an attack from alien death rays is to seek immediate shelter. Some degree of discrimination must be demonstrated in what you choose to hide behind. Death rays are capable of slicing through most buildings, but the majority of a death ray's energy is dissipated on the surface of the object it hits. Therefore, if a ray hits the outer wall of a building, it must burn through that before it can hit an inner wall. Death rays have only limited ability to penetrate to any great depth through many solid materials unless the beam is concentrated on the one spot for an extended period. As this will rarely happen in the chaos of a combat situation, the safest shelters are the ones with the thickest barriers. If you must take temporary shelter behind less substantial barricades, you may sustain severe burns if you are in direct contact with a heat conductive material. There is also the danger that the material you are sheltering behind is combustible and may ignite under

the intense heat of the death ray. If you're in an enclosed location, you must also consider the toxic fumes that may be given off by any such fire. Again, the best refuge during a death ray attack is underground.

TREATING BURNS

If aliens score a direct hit with a death ray, you're a goner, but there is a good chance that you could survive superficial burns and minor flesh wounds resulting from exposure to burning material close to the point of impact. This will, of course, depend on the nature and extent of the injuries and the availability of timely medical attention. Medical service may be in limited supply or completely unavailable during an invasion, and any time lost seeking help will definitely impact your chances of safely getting to a remote location. Yet, leaving burns or other injuries untreated may result in life-threatening infections. It's a choice that can only be made when all the factors in a situation are fully considered, and that can't be done until after the event.

HOW TO SPOT AN ALIEN REPLICANT

Aliens may not necessarily adopt the dramatic "shock and awe" approach to an invasion. A subtler "thief in the night" type of technique is equally likely to be employed by our extraterrestrial foes. If science-fiction films have taught us anything, it is that one day we may awake to discover that our friends, family members, and neighbors have been replaced by sinister alien replicants. Hatched like seeds from a pod (and thus sometimes referred to as "pod people"), these duplicates are physically indistinguishable from their human counterparts. Possessing the ability to mimick our every move, they are ostensibly normal, but are secretly at work to replace the entire human race, one individual at a time. The following tips will not only help you avoid being replaced by a mindless clone, but may also prevent you from dating one.

SEEK AND DESTROY THE PODS

Pod people usually propagate and develop while their human victim sleeps. They pass through a number of grotesque metamorphic stages before finally hatching as a carbon copy of the original human. The original is killed and disposed of soon afterward by the replicant, often with the help of other pod people. Pods are generally hidden in inconspicuous locations—like basements, attics, and the bottoms of swimming pools—usually no more than one hun-

dred feet away from their victims. These organic cocoons are the same size as their victims and consist of a semitranslucent, latex-like material that has been known to gently pulsate.

Pod people are at their most vulnerable and are easily eliminated at the larval stage. Rupturing the pod or exposing the undeveloped replicant to direct sunlight is all that is usually required to kill it. Those with a more creative bent may use any variety of weapons to do the job, from common garden shed tools to homemade incendiary devices. Make sure you keep an eye out for other pod people, as they often guard the developing replicants. They pose far more of a threat to your safety, and they are significantly more difficult to decommission.

TRUST YOUR INSTINCTS

How many times have you heard someone say, "He just doesn't seem like himself today," or "I don't know what it is, but there's something different about him"? Gut reactions should never be ignored. If something seems strange or out of place, it's usually because there's something sinister afoot. You may not be the first to notice that someone is acting weird, but you will probably be the only one who knows that he or she is an alien imposter. Those who fail to act immediately do so at their own—and humanity's—peril.

KNOW THE SIGNS

Although pod people are physically identical to their human counterparts, they do bear a number of distinguishing characterisitics.

Lack of Emotions

Do your co-workers' faces remain expressionless after you've told them your best jokes? It may not be the poor quality of your humor that's to blame. Pod people are emotionless drones, devoid of personality and devoted to propogating their own kind. Check their "emotional reflexes" by doing something bizarre, unexpected, or inappropriate, like throwing a punch, screaming obscenities, or making a lewd pass, then watch their responses carefully.

Monotone Voice

Tedious speech patterns are not the sole domain of our political leaders. Pod people are incapable of speaking in anything but a flat, deadpan voice. Their voices are often stilted and lacking in intonation. If you think "boring delivery," think "pod person."

Vacant Eyes

We have all had the experience of awakening from a daydream to find ourselves unwittingly staring at somebody across the room. This experience is often unnerving for both parties. The average person blinks approximately ten times each minute. This can increase to as much as 150 times a minute when we are nervous or being untruthful. If the guy next to you in the train blinks anything less than two times a minute, start running.

Lack of Social Skills

Our daily interactions with others can be upredictable, complicated, and, at times, confusing. Humans are masters at the subtle variations in behavior required to survive in a wide variety of social situations. We intuitively take cues from our social context, adapting our actions to maintain the fine balance between being accepted or rejected by our peers. Although pod people absorb the conscious memories of their victims, they fail to gain the intuitive reflexes required to always respond appropriately to the nuances of complex social interactions. Watch out for anyone who stands a little bit too close, laughs a little bit too long or hard, doesn't swing her arms when she walks, or forgets to put clothes on before going to work. Telltale signs such as these may indicate that you are dealing with a pod person.

UNHEEDED WARNINGS

Don't be surprised when you alert authorities to humanity's impending doom and they do not take you seriously. You will probably be ignored or referred for psychiatric assessment. When you hear clinicians in white lab coats whispering things about delusional paranoia or mass hysteria, take it as a sign that your suspicions are correct. You know the drill. You must do whatever it takes to save humanity from the insidious scourge they are so loathe to acknowledge.

POST-ABDUCTION SYNDROME

Post-Abduction Syndrome is a condition, closely related to Post-Traumatic Stress Disorder, that affects people who have had an alien abduction experience. It is characterized by increased levels of anxiety, unexplained feelings of hopelessness and dread, avoidance of or emotional reactions to things that remind them of the incident, and repression of memories associated with the abduction.

PARTING WORDS

Humanity is no stranger to visitations from other worlds. We have been the focus of extraterrestrial scrutiny since the very dawn of time. The threat of alien abduction is as real as it ever has been. Yet now, for the first time in human history, we have an opportunity to turn the tide of oppression against our celestial nemesis and reclaim

THE ALIEN INVASION SURVIVAL HANDBOOK

FACT FILE # *020729HR-20*

FACT FILE NAME: *The Drake Equation*

INCIDENT REPORT:

The Drake Equation was created in 1960 by Dr. Frank Drake (who now serves as Emeritus Professor of Astronomy and Astrophysics at the University of California, Santa Cruz) in an effort to estimate the number of ███████ extraterrestrial civilizations that may exist in our galaxy.

$$N = R^* \; f_p \times n_e \times f_l \times f_i \times f_c \times L$$

The terms in the Drake Equation are:

N = number of advanced civilizations in the galaxy

R^* = rate at which suitable stars are formed

f_p = fraction of stars with planetary systems

n_e = number of Earth-like planets per system

f_l = fraction of Earth-like planets that develop life

f_i = fraction Earth-like planets that develop intelligent life

f_c = fraction of civilizations that invent communication technology

L = lifetime of an advanced civilization

Depending on what figures are used to make this calculation, we may expect a long-distance call from anywhere between one and ten ███████ alien civilizations at some time in humanity's future.

what is rightfully ours—planet Earth. It's time to unite, as a species, and take out the intergalactic trash.

The knowledge you have gained from reading this manual has equipped you to join the growing throng of human resistance. You can feel confident that when you come face-to-face with these alien miscreants, you now have the necessary skills to defend both yourself and your family. Whether you are at the office, playing a round of golf, or on the way home from a turn through your local fast-food drive-thru, you can fend off an alien attack with both ruthless efficiency and panache.

We must not, however, take victory for granted. We must never let down our guard. We must, at all times, be ready to swing into action. The price of freedom is eternal vigilance. For, the battle will not be over until the last alien is neatly zipped into a body bag.

Whether you want to believe it or not, the information in this book is true. How you respond to it is important. Your life and the future of humanity may depend on it.

A BRIEF HISTORY OF RESISTANCE

CHAPTER SUMMARY

The complete history of the encounters between aliens and humankind is beyond the scope of this book. Many stories are already well documented, while others have been lost to the ravages of time, or have been explained away by academics as the rantings of deranged minds. However, it is important to document previously unpublished accounts and instances where the insidious plans of our alien adversaries have been thwarted by both planned and inadvertent human actions. For it is by learning from the past that we can avoid repeating it. These are stories of human courage and ingenuity in the face of unexpected circumstances and often overwhelming odds. Even though the stories recorded here represent only a small portion of humanity's successful resistance, they serve as reminders to us all that we must be ready at any moment to face our alien nemesis.

A.D. 106, ROME, ITALY

In early September 2003, workmen renovating a long disused cellar in a rectory outside of Naples, Italy, unearthed a box containing a bundle of old manuscripts. Museum staff were called and soon pronounced that they had discovered the missing annals of the Roman historian Cornelius Tacitus. Among this priceless collection were a number of personal letters, including one from the author's cousin Markus Quintus Sentius, the private secretary of the prominent Roman senator Lucius Julius Turannius. One letter includes an account of the celebrations ordered by Emperor Trajan after the defeat of Dacia in A.D. 106. The festivities lasted 123 days, during which time ten thousand gladiators fought and eleven thousand animals were butchered.

Dear Cousin,

I accompanied the Senator to the colosseum today, where we viewed the animal exhibits prior to the day's performance. The caged animals from the provinces were most striking. Lions, bears, tigers, an elephant and giraffe, all destined for death in the arena. What captured my attention, though, was the display of oddities and freaks from Cyrenaica and Aegyptus. A calf with two heads, a man with an extra arm, and a giant of monstrous proportions. There was one wretched creature, wizened and deformed, hardly human. The public were kept at a distance from its enclosure and warned that it had magical powers that could render a man unconscious. I stood transfixed by its enormous eyes, until prompted to move on by a guard.

I do not, as a rule, enjoy the games. I find them most distasteful. They cater to the common man's basest desire for blood. But I have never been one to resist displays of the supernatural and resolved to keep my eye open to see how this creature fared in battle that very afternoon.

I did not have long to wait. During the luncheon interval, the creature was dragged into the arena on a long tether. Two lightly clad gladiators approached with trident and net, but before getting within striking distance, they dropped to the earth as if dead. A murmur of surprise arose from the crowd. Another gladiator, wearing mail, leggings, a helmet, and wielding a heavy sword, came at it from behind. But within three paces, he collapsed at its feet as well. This certainly gained the attention of the spectators, who had now begun returning to their seats. They started abusing the fallen gladiators and demanding real men to slay the beast, which remained, throughout, crouched motionless, close to the ground.

The onslaught continued, gladiator after gladiator falling before the creature until it could barely be seen behind the bodies. The crowd was incredulous that so many could be defeated without a single blow falling and were suspicious that it may be just a pantomime. They bayed for blood, outraged that their wishes were being mocked. At last, the morning's champion, Manius Dentatus, entered to rapturous applause. Keeping his distance from the creature, he seized a javelin and hurled it, without ceremony, into its back. It toppled over on its side, dead. Unsheathing his dagger, Manius removed the creature's bulbous head, plunged it on a pike, and paraded it around the arena, much to the crowd's pleasure. One by one, the fallen gladiators arose from the ground, dazed and heckled by the crowd. All were publicly executed before nightfall. Manius was crushed in an incident involving two elephants the following day.

1648, JAPAN

In the year 1648, Toyotomi Yoshiro, a one-time student of the famed Japanese swordsman Miyamoto Musashi, turned from the ways of the sword and devoted himself to the austere disciplines of Zen Buddhism. He retreated to a remote monastery in the foothills of Kyoto and dedicated himself to the mastery of meditation. Zazen, one of the core principles of Zen Buddhism, involves

THE ALIEN INVASION SURVIVAL HANDBOOK

FACT FILE # *19731XV-03*

FACT FILE NAME: *Alien Encounters During the Middle Ages*

INCIDENT REPORT:

Although the existence of UFOs only became widely publicized toward the end of World War II, accounts of the phenomenon itself have appeared throughout recorded history. Some of the first ▓▓▓▓▓▓▓ encounters were reported in newspapers from sixteenth-century Europe. Two accounts are given below.

1566, BASEL, SWITZERLAND

Shortly after dawn on August 7, 1566, the citizens of Basel, Switzerland, witnessed "many large, black spheres ... moving before the sun at great speed and striking against each other as if in ▓▓▓▓▓ battle. Many of them became red and fiery, and afterwards faded and died out," writes Samuel Coccius in the local newspaper the day after the incident.

1561, NUREMBERG, GERMANY

Just after sunrise on April 14, 1561, there was a "very dreadful spectacle" over the city of Nuremberg, Germany. The sky filled with cylindrical ▓▓▓▓▓ objects from which spheres emerged. Crosses "the color of blood" and tubes resembling cannon barrels also appeared, whereupon the objects "began to fight one another." This remarkable display continued for more than an hour, then came to an end when the objects abruptly fell from the sky.

practitioners sitting on the floor and concentrating on their breathing or on koans (paradoxical statements or riddles with no logical answer, such as "What is the sound of one hand clapping?") to calm the mind and body in order the gain some insight into the nature of personal existence.

Once a month, it was tradition at the monastery to hold a sesshin, or seven-day period of intensive meditation. On one such occasion, Yoshiro arose three hours before the other monks for a time of quiet, personal reflection. Sitting on the temple floor beside a small fire, he noticed a flash of light in the night sky. Some time later, sensing a presence, he turned and saw what seemed to be three small, naked children standing in the doorway. Without a sound, they pounced at him. Old habits, however, die hard with a warrior. Without breaking his meditative concentration, he instinctively sprung to his feet and grabbed two hot fire pokers. Brandishing them like bokkens (traditional Japanese wooden swords), he felled two of the intruders with a swift volley of blows to their heads, which, being so large, were easy targets. The third turned and silently scurried off into the night.

Upon closer inspection of the bodies, Yoshiro noted in his journal, "They were both pale and unfed, with heads misshapen through some sorcery of birth. Although dead, their eyes, large and black, seemed to follow me still."

Yoshiro presented the bodies to the monastery's abbot, who acknowledged their unnatural origin. They were ritually sun-dried and bound for preservation. For the next 297 years, the bodies were periodically put on display during religious festivals and used to warn novice monks of the dangers of sorcery. Both the temple and the bodies were destroyed by a stray Allied bomb during an air raid in 1945.

1804, LEWIS AND CLARK EXPEDITION

The Lewis and Clark expedition across North America remains one of the greatest exploratory endeavors of all time. With thirty-three men, they managed to cross more than 8,000 miles of unmapped territory over a period of twenty-eight months.

A missing journal entry, apparently misplaced during storage in the last century, was discovered in late 1997 during renovations at Thomas Jefferson's private retreat, Poplar Forest, near Lynchburg, Virginia. The following is an undated excerpt from the journal entry.

At half past three, our progress was interrupted by the approach of a violent thunderstorm from the N.E.

On the evening of the 25th, the party halted and encamped on the upper point of the small island that lies close to the village to which we had been invited to visit the previous day. A small, armed party was formed and suitable gifts prepared. Upon landing on the shore, we were received with elegant painted buffalo robes and carried to the village by six men apiece. We were not permitted to touch the ground until we were put down inside the grand council lodge. After smoking, a hearty supper, and much dissertation, we exchanged gifts and prepared to retire to our boat. The chiefs requested that we would not leave them so soon and invited us to view a solemn ceremony to be held that night as a sign of their good will. Although we were fatigued and reluctant, they implored us with such sincerity that we decided to accept their gracious invitation and followed them out of the village. As we walked, our interpreters explained that we were to witness a coming-of-age ceremony. The Indians believed the sky to be the residence of unusual spirits who were periodically offered boys who were of age, to be taken away to receive the markings of manhood.

Three boys were handsomely dressed for the occasion and led the procession between the raised burial mounds of their ancestors to a small clearing, ringed with large stones. We were directed to remain outside the circle as the boys were led into its center by one of the chiefs. There followed a long and elaborate ceremony, employing both dance and song. Plagued by a horde of troublesome mosquitoes, we were about to take our leave when the Sergeant of the Guard drew our attention to a bright light in the northern sky. Upon seeing it, the Indians became very excited, withdrawing away from the circle and motioning us to follow them towards the woods. The three boys were left standing alone in the center of the circle. The light, which at first glance appeared as some manifestation of the northern lights, approached, then retreated a number of times before coming to rest over the stone circle. We could now see clearly that the light emanated from some form of solid object that floated, motionless, above the boys. My men were greatly disturbed by this apparition and were keen to ready their weapons for action. Our Indian hosts beseeched us to remain silent and warned of displeasing the visitors.

We watched as the object descended to within an arm's reach of the boys. Before our very eyes, the three youths fell to the ground as if dead. This greatly troubled my men, one of whom discharged his weapon. The object, within an instant, rose a furlong vertically, and then disappeared at a remarkable speed towards the eastern horizon.

Our hosts were greatly upset by this turn of events and suggested, in no uncertain terms, that we leave immediately. As we took our leave, we noted the boys had risen and were standing dazed and bewildered within the stone circle. Upon returning to the boat, the men would only say that it was a bad omen. All have since refused to speak of the incident.

1826, NORTHWEST FRONTIER

Josiah Johnson was known as the "gentleman trapper," having left his native England for the wilds of the American frontier to work with Hudson's Bay Company in the early 1800s. It was not uncommon for Johnson to spend two or three seasons in the wilderness

THE ALIEN INVASION SURVIVAL HANDBOOK

FACT FILE # *081030XF-10*

FACT FILE NAME: *Mystery Airships*

INCIDENT REPORT:

During the late 1890s, a wave of mysterious UFO sightings was widely reported in the press across the United States. Tens of thousands of Americans were convinced they had sighted large, fast-flying ███████ airships unlike any technology available in the day. They were typically described as being cigar-shaped and were capable of extraordinary speeds and midair maneuvers. Sightings were also reported from as far afield as Europe and New Zealand.

One report in the Dallas Morning Star recounts an incident in Aurora, Texas, in which an airship crashed into a local windmill, killing the pilot, who was described as being not of this world. The craft itself was constructed of an unknown lightweight alloy. Sections of the ███████ airship were also engraved with indecipherable hieroglyphic symbols. The pilot was eventually buried in the town cemetery. UFO researchers discovered the headstone marking the grave in the early 1970s, but when they returned a few years later, they found that the headstone and remains had disappeared.

before bringing his furs into Fort Vancouver for sale. After one profitable year, he met a newspaper reporter in a local bordello. He recounted the following story, which was subsequently published in the *Boston Courier* later that year.

After having set his final trap for the day, Johnson had not gone more than fifty paces when he heard it snap shut, followed by a high-pitched squealing. Thinking he had caught an animal, he went to investigate. Arriving at the trap site, he was surprised to find what looked like a small, naked, malnourished child.

The newspaper quoted Johnson's account: "Its skin was the color of a three-day-old corpse, with spindly limbs. Its head was deformed through some defect of birth, with eyes as large and as black as a newborn calf. Oh, how the creature did wail. In a fashion that made me grit my teeth and cover my ears."

He immediately approached the creature with the intent of freeing its leg, which had been almost severed beneath the knee. As he neared, he was overcome by a "fainting spell" and collapsed. When he revived, both the creature and the trap had disappeared. Although a skilled tracker, he was unable to find any trace of the creature. He did, however, notice curious scorch marks on the tree trunks high above his head.

Johnson could not be further questioned about the incident, as he returned to his camp the following day. He died of suspected food poisoning two months later.

1845, KING WILLIAM ISLAND, CANADIAN ARCTIC

In late August 2003, an oil company reconnaissance team recovered a metal canister buried under a rock cairn on King William Island in northern Canada. It contained a number of poorly preserved documents and some weathered European and Inuit artifacts. After

extensive preservation work by a private antiquities company in
Ontario, it was discovered that the document was a journal extract
by the self-professed last surviving member of the ill-fated Northwest Passage expedition of 1845, led by a former lieutenant-gov-
ernor of Van Diemen's Land, Sir John Franklin. The unnamed author recounts many of the previously known facts of the mission,
including their ship's entrapment in sea ice in Victoria Strait for
more than a year, and half the expedition's team dying from disease
and starvation. He also recounts how the remaining survivors, thir-
ty-five men in total, had embarked on a perilous overland journey
in an attempt to reach the nearest Western outpost, on the Great
Slave Lake, several hundred miles to the south. What was unexpected was the author's account of the disappearance of the surviving members of the party after the appearance of strange lights in
the pre-dawn sky.

> Most curious they were. At first we thought them a manifestation of the aurora
> borealis. Moving hither and yon at a startling pace. Those of us who were awake
> watched the spectacle in silent awe. The natives who had camped beside us
> were most alarmed at the sight and proceeded to decamp immediately, urging
> us to do the same. Being our best hope yet of survival, I beseeched them to tarry,
> but to no avail. They set off towards the southeast and were soon swallowed by
> the dark. I hastened in pursuit, hoping to appease their fear. I had not struggled
> more than a mile headlong into a stout breeze, when I glanced up to see a figure
> in front of me. I fell to ground, unable to move and barely able to breathe. Watch-
> ing the figure approach out of the night, I could see that it was unclothed and
> wasted. It was almost upon me when I heard a dull thud and a horrible shriek
> that rose above the shrill wind. The figure fell to its knees and then onto its face,
> whereupon I could see a harpoon embedded in its back. The natives had re-
> turned for me, hastening past the body at a distance, and carried me with them
> towards the south. I believe I owe my life to their rescue and shall forever remain

indebted to them. We returned to our camp in the light of day, but it was desert-
ed. There were signs of a skirmish, but there were no tracks leading away from
the encampment apart from ours. The natives all the while watched the sky with
a genuine fear. With a great sense of urgency, they implored me to collect what
I could of my belongings so we could depart. I remonstrated that we should
search for the crew but they …

The rest of the page is missing. What can be read of the last entry
of the journal tells of the author's journey with the Inuit and their
preparation to make a hazardous open-water crossing. Although
the details of the writer's fate remain a mystery, we do know that
he never reached the Great Slave Lake settlement.

1862, RICHMOND, VIRGINIA

Confederate captain Uriah Smith, working under orders from Gen.
Joseph E. Johnston, lead a small company of Confederate soldiers
on a nocturnal reconnaissance mission behind Union lines during the two-day Battle of Seven Pines. Three hours before dawn,
they spotted what they thought was one of the Union's aerostats,
or manned surveillance balloons, positioned over a nearby hillside.
Smith's story is as follows:

We saw it through the trees, at first. Shaped more like an upturned bowl than a
balloon. Larger and more graceful than the balloons we saw yesterday. It hung
there for some time and then started drifting toward us. Thinking it had broken
free of its moorings, we waited to see where it would go. It stopped over a small
clearing not more than two chains away and alighted as gentle as a feather. It
was a solid structure, the color of polished iron in the moonlight. Hiding in a
thicket, we watched as a door opened and its occupants came out. Children, by
what we could see; four of them. Thinking that we might capture them, I gave
the command for the men to ready their weapons, whereupon the Union Balloon

Corps men, hearing us, instantly turned and ran toward us with a speed and agility that was frightening. We opened fire, seeming to hit one before they all disappeared into the undergrowth. Shortly after, the balloon rose into the air and flew off toward the east so quickly that it was out of sight within moments.

Both Captain Smith and his men returned unscathed to their camp. Captain Smith survived the war and worked as a postmaster in Raleigh, North Carolina, for the next twenty years.

1888, EQUATORIA, AFRICA

Sir Henry Morton Stanley was a Welsh-born explorer and journalist. He is most remembered for his 1867 expedition, commissioned by the *New York Herald*, to search for the missing Scottish explorer David Livingstone in central Africa.

After a journey plagued by disease, desertions, and insurrection, Stanley found Livingstone on the shores of Lake Tanganyika, in present-day Tanzania, were he uttered the immortal greeting "Dr. Livingstone, I presume?"

After a number of subsequent, well-publicized expeditions in Sub-Saharan Africa, Stanley returned again in 1887 to lead the ill-fated mission to "rescue" the governor of Equatoria, in present-day Sudan. In a previously unpublished journal entry, Stanley records:

May 27, 1888

Being yet again short on fresh provisions, I resolved to lead a hunting party to shoot some game. Sporting my Starr Carbine, with two porters carrying my 12-bore 'bone crusher' and a further supply of ammunition, I headed northwest from our camp towards a narrow, marshy ravine at the base of a conical hill, on whose slopes flourished a dense thicket. I had seen three fine, plump antelope there the previous day and hoped to bag one for our evening meal. We crept cautiously along, looking keenly into every dark opening for the glint of an eye, but, alas, we saw nothing.

After an hour's search, we came to a mire, overgrown with dense reeds and papyrus. Crossing this quagmire, we sunk up to our waists in foul-smelling ooze. Here we were again plagued by the ubiquitous sword fly and tsetse that had made so much of this journey a misery.

There was a sudden movement in the vegetation lining the shore. Suspecting an ambush by hostile natives or a crocodile, I opened fire. Although I could see no target, luck was with me and I hit my mark. There was a wild thrashing in the rushes, a hideous wail, and then silence.

We dragged ourselves out of the black mud and, still covered in slime, came around our quarry from behind. Taking my double-barreled gun from Mabruki, we entering a small clearing in the rushes. A frightful sight lay before us, which still haunts me to this day. A small, albino native child, frightfully disfigured, with a swollen head and large, protruding eyes, lay naked in front of us. Its arms were disproportionately long and it was missing a finger from each hand. A vicious head wound seeped a dark, viscous fluid, not blood, onto the reeds around its head. My porters were aghast at the sight. They both stepped back, wide eyed, in abject horror. "Utami. Utami," they murmured, then looked up warily at the sky.

My attention was instead averted to a thick clump of undergrowth to my right. Two more of these God-forsaken creatures, for one could hardly call them human, emerged with a startling ferocity. My porters shrieked and ran for cover, leaving me alone, not more than ten yards from the two swiftly approaching demonic forms. I instinctively sprang back, almost tripping on the ammunition dropped by the hastily retreating porters.

Although unarmed, the creatures' intentions were unmistakably hostile. Throwing the barrel of the gun into my left hand, I fired, hitting one in the shoulder. With its arm hanging by nothing more than a thread, it dropped to the ground with a blood-curdling scream. The other stopped momentarily, assessing the situation, then advanced towards me in a stealthy, sidelong manner. Its villainous eyes locked on mine like a spider courting its prey. With one round left, I aimed the muzzle of my gun at its face and ordered it to stop. It paid no heed, suddenly launching itself towards me at a frightful speed. I discharged my weapon, and the shot, true to its aim, ripped through the creature's head, throwing its lifeless form to the ground.

I approached the vile creature with the shoulder wound, which had now slipped into unconsciousness, and, in an act of mercy, hastily drew my keen, sharp-edged knife across its throat.

That evening, around the campfire, I learned that Utami is the native word for "sky man," a mythical being that stole their children and took them into the clouds. I went back at dawn for a second look, but the bodies had gone, taken by lions during the night, no doubt.

1982, UKRAINE

Vladimir Razumovsky, a twenty-seven-year-old factory worker from the industrial city of Kremenchuk, Ukraine, walked home late one night after celebrating a colleague's birthday. He lived just out of town in a small cottage his grandmother had left to him after her death. He had just bought a new Walkman at the party from a friend's black market contact and fell inebriated on his bed listening to the only tape he had, *The Essential Jimi Hendrix, Volume One*. At just after three in the morning, with the pounding beat of "Voodoo Child" playing through his headphones, he awoke to find several dark figures leaning over him. He screamed in fright, thinking he had disturbed thieves and would be killed and found dead floating in the local channel the next morning. The intruders, startled by the scream, stumbled away from the bed, tripping over assorted boxes and piles of dirty laundry on the floor.

THE ALIEN INVASION SURVIVAL HANDBOOK

FACT FILE # *19737XR-18*

FACT FILE NAME: *The Rendlesham Forest Incident*

INCIDENT REPORT:

On the night of December 26, 1980, an unidentified flying object was reported by security officers near the Royal Air Force base at Woodbridge, in the county of Suffolk, England. At first, thinking that they may have seen an ▬▬▬▬▬▬▬ aircraft crash, the officers entered the forest adjacent to the base to investigate. There, they witnessed an oval-shaped object, "like an eye," hovering in the mist above a clearing. It was metallic in appearance, measured approximately 10 feet across, and glowed—illuminating the surrounding forest. As they approached, the object maneuvered between the trees and disappeared. Animals in the vicinity were reported to "go crazy with fear" during the incident.

After returning to their base, the patrolmen filed a report and were instructed by their superiors not to speak of the incident. However, the story was leaked to the press and received front-page coverage on national newspapers. The servicemen returned to the clearing the following day and found scorch marks on surrounding trees and three small indentations forming a triangular ▬▬▬▬▬ pattern on the ground.

The Rendlesham Forest incident is perhaps the most famous UFO sighting to have happened in Britain and ranks amongst the best-known UFO events worldwide.

movsky reached to his bedside table and grabbed an empty e of vodka, which he hurled at the intruders, hitting one in the ce. The terrified Razumovsky continued screaming and throwing anything he could get his hands on in the dark. The intruders beat a hasty retreat out of his bedroom and headed through the kitchen toward the back door with Razumovsky, now feeling more confident, in hot pursuit. Grabbing an iron, he swung it around his head like an Olympic hammer thrower and heaved it with all his might. The cord wrapped around one of the intruder's legs, like Spanish boleadoras, sending him sprawling onto the floor. Razumovsky, unable to stop in time, tripped on the prone figure, landing on top of him. Razumovsky's recollections of what happened next are somewhat hazy, but a brief tussle ensued, blows were exchanged, and then the intruders were gone. Razumovsky stood and screamed some abuse about the intruders' mother as they headed across the field on the other side of the road.

He turned his Walkman off and was about to close the door when a bright light caught his eye. There in the paddock, not more than 100 yards from his cottage, was a large, luminescent, disc-shaped craft that lifted silently into the night sky. It hovered momentarily over the field, sending sheep blahing in all directions, took off at a tremendous speed toward the east, and was gone.

Razumovsky made an official report at the local police office on the way to work the next day. A number of other people—including a truck driver, two shift workers, and a night patrolman—also reported seeing a fast-moving light early that morning.

The report was filed and forgotten, until it was discovered by researchers after the collapse of the Soviet Union. Razumovsky was contacted for the writing of this handbook and recounted the incident exactly as he had reported it twenty-five years ago.

1998, QUEENSTOWN, NEW ZEALAND

The case of Rangi Tui, a thirty-four-year-old seasonal sheepshearer from the South Island of New Zealand, highlights, yet again, the diverse range of anti-electroparalysis techniques that have been successfully employed in resisting alien abduction.

Tui had spent Saturday night at the local tavern celebrating his team's win in a rugby match that afternoon. By 2 a.m., festivities had started to die down, and as he was expected at work early the next morning, he decided to head back to his lodgings for a few hours of sleep before an early 6 a.m. start. He offered Chris Hayman, a twenty-four-year-old co-worker, a lift back to the sheep station, some 20 miles out of town.

By the time Tui reached the gate of the property, Hayman had fallen asleep on the backseat. Tui started driving up the two-mile rough dirt track over rolling hills to the shearers' quarters.

As Tui proceeded up the track, he saw what he thought was the headlight of a motorcycle heading toward him. He initially thought it must have been the property owner "out possum shootin'," but as the light approached, he was surprised to see it rise up into the night sky. Confused, he stopped the car and tried, unsuccessfully, to wake the inebriated Hayman. Tui strained to keep his eyes on the light but lost sight of it as it rose directly over the car. It was difficult to judge its size, but it appeared to be at least as big as the car he was driving. He jumped out and looked up, but the light was nowhere to be seen. Scanning the sky and seeing nothing, he took a few moments to relieve himself and was about to get back into the car when he was suddenly surrounded by an intense beam of light. Thinking someone had turned a spotlight on him, he remonstrated, yelling, "Come on, you jokers, turn that fucking thing off!" Shielding

THE ALIEN INVASION SURVIVAL HANDBOOK

FACT FILE # *16739XM-14*

FACT FILE NAME: *Cattle Mutilation*

INCIDENT REPORT:

Cattle mutilation is a puzzling phenomenon that some believe has been unequivocally linked to extraterrestrial ████████ activity. This phenomenon is characterized by the untimely and often gruesome deaths of our uddered friends, usually under circumstances that defy reasonable explanation. Carcasses exhibit surgically precise incisions and can be wholly drained of blood, often with specific internal organs deftly removed. Sometimes multiple carcasses have been found arranged in bizarre geometric formations in open fields. The crime scene is always devoid of any evidence, including footprints, tire marks, blood, or any of the usual telltale signs of wholesale slaughter. These macabre massacres can also occur in remarkably short periods of time. In 1983, one Minnesotan dairy farmer left his herd unattended for twenty minutes to make a phone call. When he returned, he found them all, save one, dead on the ground, with their bellies neatly opened up like a high-school biology experiment. The one living cow was found quietly chewing its cud on the roof of a nearby milking shed.

Aliens also seem to have a disquieting penchant for mammalian genitalia, often removing said ████████ appendages but leaving the rest of the beast intact. Why they possess this obsession with reproductive organs is

anyone's guess. But when we consider our own species'
predilection for the assorted body parts of our fellow
sentient beings, it's hardly surprising that aliens may
also share some bizarre and inexplicable habits.

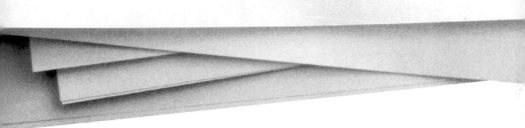

his eyes from the light, he looked up and could make out the dark
outline of a large object some 150 feet directly above him. He felt
an intense burst of heat on his face and then blacked out, dropping
to the ground.

As Tui regained consciousness, he became aware of movement
around him. His eyes were closed, but he felt a bright light still
shining in his face. He attempted to cover his face with his hands,

but they didn't move. He tried to scream, but couldn't. He was paralyzed. Tui could only just open his eyes against the intense glare and make out the forms of several dark shapes leaning over him. He immediately thought that he must have been in an accident and was now in a hospital emergency room. As his eyes adjusted to the light, he saw that the figures standing over him looked like creatures from a science-fiction movie, with bulging heads, large eyes, and spindly limbs.

Tui was horrified by what he saw, but was powerless to react. The aliens continued about their business, much of which was just outside Tui's field of vision. He did notice one of the aliens handling what looked like a chrome-plated hand drill, and within moments, he felt an excruciating pain in his lower leg. The pain crept up his limb like tendrils of lava until he thought he was going to pass out again, when it eased off abruptly. Tui's sense of helplessness soon turned to rage as the pain surged through his leg a second time. The words of an ancient Māori battle song—the haka, which is often performed by New Zealanders prior to playing rugby matches—filled his mind.

Ka mate! Ka mate! Ka ora! Ka ora!	I die! I die! I live! I live!
Ka mate! Ka mate! Ka ora! Ka ora!	I die! I die! I live! I live!
Tenei te tangata puhuru huru	This is the hairy man
Nana nei i tiki mai	Who fetched the Sun
Whakawhiti te ra	And caused it to shine again
A upa ne! ka upa ne!	One upward step! Another upward step!
A upane kaupane whiti te ra!	An upward step, another … the Sun shines!
Hi !!!	

As Tui focused on the aggressive intension of the chant, the pain seemed to abate. He repeated it over and over, and he slowly felt sensation returning to his fingertips, then his arms. He opened his eyes again and saw that the aliens had stopped what they were doing and were just staring expressionlessly at him. He could hear the words of the haka coming from his own mouth now. His paralysis was gone. The aliens seemed alarmed. He sprang to his feet, still a little unsteady, and noticed that he was naked. He looked down and saw a metallic hose protruding from his lower leg. He ripped it out and pounced on the alien wielding the drill, knocking the creature to the floor with a single blow to its face. He elbowed the alien behind him in the chest and could hear the sickening crack of bones as it dropped. Having been involved in more than a few pub brawls in his time, Tui knew he shouldn't hold anything back. He grabbed a third alien by the neck and leg and rammed it headfirst into the wall, then it dropped motionless on the deck.

The three other aliens left standing in the room did not come to their fallen comrades' aid, but hastily retreated through a doorway on the other side of the examination table. As they left the room, the door began to slide down. Tui vaulted over the examination bench and rolled under the door just as it was closing.

The aliens were scurrying up a passage to his left. Tui gave chase, pounding two more to the deck from behind. The last one was only a few yards away, running panic-stricken toward a translucent wall at the end of the corridor. Tui thought he had it cornered. Tui was about to strike when the alien disappeared straight through the shimmering wall. It solidified as the alien passed through it, and Tui slammed heavily into the now-solid wall. Shaken, he sat reeling on the deck. Then, hearing a noise behind him, he turned to see a hatch open a few yards back up the corridor. He staggered over and looked down, only to see trees passing swiftly some 30 feet below in the dim light of dawn.

He received a sudden sharp jab in his back and fell forward, out of the hatch. As he plummeted, he saw the large, silver-gray, metallic, disc-shaped craft he had just fallen out of shoot upward and disappear behind a cloud.

Tui landed heavily in a freshly raked sand trap in the Royal Golf Course in Rotorua, on the North Island, and passed out. He came to at the sound of a stern voice above him. Early-morning golfers had found him naked and unconscious and called the police.

After being questioned at the local police station, he was provided with a new set of clothes and released without charge, but with a warning. The interviewing officer, Constable Barry Goodmead, put the incident down to excessive drinking, but was unable to explain how Tui had traveled from Queenstown to Rotorua in just two hours. Tui, unable to live the story down, emigrated to Australia two years later and now works in a meat-packing factory near Bega, on the south coast of New South Wales.

REFERENCES & RESOURCES

WEBSITES

WWW.UFOEVIDENCE.ORG One of the Internet's largest sources of research and information on the UFO phenomenon.

WWW.UFOCASEBOOK.COM A popular information source on UFOs.

WWW.ABOVETOPSECRET.COM A popular conspiracy theory website.

WWW.UFOS-ALIENS.CO.UK One of Europe's largest UFO websites.

WWW.MUFON.COM Mutual UFO Network

WWW.CUFOS.ORG The Dr. J. Allen Hynek Center for UFO Studies

WWW.NARCAP.ORG National Aviation Reporting Center on Anomalous Phenomena

WWW.NICAP.ORG National Investigations Committee on Aerial Phenomena

BOOKS & ARTICLES

U.S. Military Manual FM 21-150: Combatives–Hand-To-Hand Combat

Mantrapping by Ragnar Benson (Paladin Press, 1981)

"How To: Turn Everyday Objects Into Weapons" by Nick Clark http://au.askmen.com/money/how_to_300/346_how_to.html

APPENDIX C:

ALIEN ENCOUNTER LOGBOOK

Make sure you fill out this logbook each time you have an alien encounter. It will act as an invaluable record of your experience and aid in assessing your vulnerability to alien abduction.

DATE:_____ TIME:_____

LOCATION:_____

OTHER WITNESSES: _____

_____

_____

_____

_____

_____

TYPE OF ENCOUNTER:

☐ 1) UFO SIGHTING

☐ 2) UFO SIGHTING WITH PHYSICAL EVIDENCE

☐ 3) ALIEN SIGHTING

☐ 4) ALIEN ABDUCTION

DETAILS:_____

_____

_____

_____

_____

_____

_____

_____

ACTION TAKEN: _____

_____

_____

_____

_____

_____

_____

BODY COUNT (IF APPLICABLE): _____

DRAWINGS AND DIAGRAMS:

INDEX

MORE GREAT TITLES FROM HOW BOOKS!

KAWAII NOT: CUTE GONE BAD BY MEGHAN MURPHY

Kawaii is the Japanese term for *cute*, as in, "look at the fuzzy kitten, he's so kawaii," and *not* is an English term meaning "not." Explore the darker side of cute with this fun comic strip collection.

ISBN: 978-1-60061-076-9, paperback, 208 p, #Z1845

100 DAYS OF MONSTERS BY STEFAN G. BUCHER

Join in on a quirky and irreverent romp through a bizarre world filled with unruly ink blot monsters based on designer and illustrator Stefan Bucher's dailymonster.com website.

ISBN: 978-1-60061-091-2, hardcover with DVD, 224 p, #Z1980

DEAR FUTURE ME: HOPES, FEARS, SECRETS, RESOLUTIONS
EDITED BY MATT SLY AND JAY PATRIKIOS CREATORS OF FUTUREME.ORG

Delve into the lives of ordinary people at their most honest. With time capsule appeal, *Dear Future Me* is an insightful collection of letters written by everyday people to their future selves.

ISBN: 978-1-58180-977-0, paperback, 256 p, #Z0790